THE ADDICTIONS HANDBOOK

Alvin, Virginia, and
Robert Silverstein

ENSLOW PUBLISHERS, INC.

Bloy St. and Ramsey Ave.	P.O. Box 38
Box 777	Aldershot
Hillside, N.J. 07205	Hants GU12 6BP
U.S.A.	U.K.

Library of Congress Cataloging-In-Publication Data

Silverstein, Alvin.
    The Addictions Handbook / Alvin, Virginia, and Robert Silverstein.
      p. cm. — (Issues in focus)
    Includes bibliographical references and index.
    Summary: Describes many different types of addictions, their
effects, and treatments.
    ISBN 0-89490-205-9
    1. Drug abuse—Juvenile literature. 2. Compulsive behavior—
Juvenile literature. I. Silverstein, Virginia B.
II. Silverstein, Robert A. III. Title. IV. Series: Issues in focus
(Hillside, N.J.)
    [DNLM: 1. Drug abuse. 2. Compulsive behavior.]
HV5801.S49 1991
362.29—dc20   90-14093
                                  CIP
                                  AC

Printed in the United States of America

10 9 8 7 6 5 4 3 2

Acknowledgements

The authors would like to thank Dr. Mark Gold, Director of Research at Fair Oaks Hospital in Summit, New Jersey, for his review of the manuscript.

THE ADDICTIONS HANDBOOK

I. INTRODUCTION

II. REFERENCE

III. EPILOGUE

INTRODUCTION

What is Addiction?

Addiction. Everybody agrees that it's a problem—one of the most serious problems facing our world today. But just what is it? What do you think of when you hear the word "addiction"?

Perhaps you picture a drug addict, crouching in a filthy room in an abandoned building as he injects heroin into his arm with a needle. The image of an alcoholic, clutching a bottle and sleeping huddled in a doorway, might come to mind. Those are unpleasant pictures, and they may seem very remote—sad fates that could happen only to someone else.

Does "addiction" suggest something closer to you? Do you see a friend who smokes one cigarette after another and has tried several times to stop? Or a parent who says, "I just don't feel human till I have my cup of coffee in the morning!" and has half a dozen more coffees and cola drinks during the day? Perhaps you think of someone who frets unless she runs five miles every day, or someone who's always working and never has time to go out with friends or take a vacation. What about someone who can't say no to ice cream and candy, or someone who's been losing a lot of money at the racetrack lately and still keeps going? Or a person who takes a pill to go to sleep and another pill to get up in the morning?

These are all images of people we might call addicted. They all share one very important thing in common—a compulsive need for something without which they cannot function properly. Although it's true that the person who runs every day might not seem to be as bad off as a heroin addict, the running addict can have a serious problem when running begins to interfere with and control his or her everyday life.

Changing Definitions

Our ideas about addiction have changed greatly over the years. The term comes from the Latin word *addicere,* which means "to favor." Today this word has taken on a much stronger connotation: "to devote" or "to surrender" oneself to something. Addicts experience a strong desire for something and then constantly give in to this desire. The need to satisfy the craving can become so strong that addicts will do things they never could have imagined before. They may lie, cheat, and steal, sacrificing treasured possessions, friendships, and even family.

At first the term *addiction* was used to describe only a physical dependence on certain types of drugs. Drugs such as opium and heroin, for example, when used for an extended time actually change the cells of the body so that a user needs regular doses of the drug just to feel normal. If the drug is withheld, the addict may suffer severe *withdrawal symptoms*—painful muscle cramps, uncontrollable shaking, nausea, and sometimes even convulsions. The addictive drugs were thought to be very different from "nonaddictive" drugs, which do not cause the body to become physically dependent and can be stopped at any time without triggering withdrawal symptoms.

Closer observation and more sophisticated knowledge of the body's biochemistry, however, gradually revealed that withdrawal symptoms are

10

only part of the story. Many drugs that were considered nonaddictive just a decade or two ago are now known to produce subtle but important changes in the brain cells. Valium and other tranquilizers, still very commonly prescribed, can be highly addictive. Cocaine, once thought to produce only a "psychological dependence," is now regarded as one of the most powerfully addictive drugs. Smoking is still considered by many people as only a "bad habit," yet then Surgeon General C. Everett Koop stated in 1988 that tobacco is "addicting in the same sense as are drugs such as heroin and cocaine."

Meanwhile, not everyone who experiments with an addictive drug becomes an addict. A large-scale study of Vietnam veterans in the mid-seventies, for example, revealed that nearly half of them had taken narcotics such as heroin and opium during their tour of duty. Some of them had become heavy users. Yet the vast majority of these men stopped using drugs when they returned to the United States. Even among the wartime addicts, only about 7 percent became readdicted in civilian life. (This low rate is in sharp contrast to the experience of drug treatment programs in the United States, where two-thirds of addicts typically go back to drugs within six months after treatment.)

Moreover, although addicts may prefer a particular drug, they will switch to another if their choice is not available and may even become addicted to substances like over-the-counter diet pills, which are not normally regarded as addictive. When "recovered" from one addiction, they may later acquire another. Abuse experts were not surprised, for example, when Kitty Dukakis went into a treatment center for alcohol abuse in 1989. She had conquered an addiction to amphetamine diet pills in 1982 but was unable to stop cigarette smoking. The stress of her husband's presidential campaign and the aftermath of its failure led to some episodes of uncontrolled drinking that alerted her to the need for help. Governor Dukakis's comment about his wife's problem could apply just as well to others: "Whether it comes in a bottle or is solid, if you're chemically dependent, you're chemically dependent."

During the 1970s and 1980s, the definition of addiction has grown still more broad. In addition to physical addiction to specific chemical substances (drugs), abuse experts now recognize that people can become psychologically dependent on certain kinds of behavior—eating, for example, or forms of exercise such as running. One "addict" may spend ten or fifteen hours a day working, every day of the week; another may put in just as many hours staring at the TV set. The common factor is that these activities, which would be normal forms of behavior if done in moderation, become compulsive. They begin to control the person's life and are continued, even when they begin to have harmful effects. A "runaholic" might persist in running in spite of muscle aches, minor sprains, or more serious injuries; if forced to stop, the running addict may suffer from irritability, depression, and other "withdrawal symptoms."

Typically, substance addiction goes hand in hand with compulsive behavior. The substance addict compulsively seeks out continued doses of the substance. But not all compulsive behavior involves substances. The compulsion to seek out certain activities can seem just as strong as the compulsion to take substances.

People tend—often unconsciously—to make value judgments about the various kinds of addictions. A person's age, income, community, and other social factors tend to color these judgments, but there are some fairly general patterns. The average person, for example, considers compulsive behavior less harmful than substance addiction—being addicted to television, let us say, is not "as bad" as being addicted to caffeine. There is also a ranking of the various substance addictions. In the popular view, addiction to caffeine (in the form of coffee, tea, or a cola drink) is not as bad as addiction to nicotine (in the form of smoking, chewing tobacco, or taking snuff). Nicotine addiction, in turn, is less frowned on than alcohol addiction; and a drinking

12

problem is not usually viewed as seriously as drug addiction—although alcohol itself is a dangerous (though legal) drug.

Some specialists object to applying the concept of addiction too loosely. They say that "sexaholism," "video game addiction," and other new addictions are just the latest pop culture gimmicks, better suited to talk shows than to serious medical concern. Yet the idea that all addictions are related is rapidly gaining acceptance. Increasingly, medical specialists are beginning to view all addictions as a single problem, or disease, expressed in different ways.

It may seem hard at first to understand how we can talk about a chemical addiction to heroin and compulsive running as different aspects of the same "addictive disease." Yet there are similarities between them, rooted in the body's chemistry. Heroin causes actual chemical changes within the body. What about running?

Researchers have discovered that running (and various other activities) stimulate the brain to produce natural pain-killers called *endorphins,* which are chemically similar to narcotics such as morphine and heroin. In addition to numbing pain, endorphins produce feelings of pleasure and well-being. Just as people can become hooked on chemical drugs that produce pleasant feelings, they can also become addicted to behaviors that generate a "high." Compulsive behavior may thus be a kind of addiction to the person's own natural drugs, the endorphins. Indeed, some specialists now define addiction as "compulsive pleasure seeking."

Stages of Addiction

Compulsive pleasure-seeking behaviors, whether they involve chemicals or activities, result in a quick "high" or feeling of euphoria. But the high fades fairly rapidly, and a "low" almost always follows. The person is then motivated to take the drug again or repeat the behavior to make the low go away.

According to Abraham Wikler, a researcher at the Federal Narcotic Hospital in Lexington, Kentucky, narcotics addiction takes place in two stages. His model is useful in examining other addictions, as well.

The first stage is the *acquisition* phase, when a person indulges in a behavior because of the pleasure found in each experience. The behavior has not yet become a compulsion at this beginning stage. The person is not yet addicted; he or she enjoys the feelings the activity or substance brings and "chooses" to seek that feeling. As the person turns to this activity more often, the body becomes more adjusted to it, and a *tolerance* builds up: more of the substance or a more intense experience is needed to feel the same "high."

Thus, we come to the next stage of addiction: the *maintenance* stage. The person's body has become used to the behavior; the highs are briefer and less intense, and the lows that follow them are so unbearable that relieving the feelings of depression or physical discomfort becomes a major motivation.

The addictive behavior now becomes the most important thing in the addicts' lives. Everything else seems less urgent. Gradually, they lose more and more control over their lives. Their relationships begin to suffer. They may be unable to function at their jobs. Their health begins to deteriorate. They're hooked on something that really no longer gives them pleasure. Yet they continue, constantly trying to feel "normal" again.

This picture synthesizes two different views of addiction. Some *addictionologists* (people who study addiction) believe that addicts become addicted to pleasure. Others argue that addiction arises as a way to avoid the withdrawal symptoms that come when an addictive behavior is stopped.

Some researchers believe that the initial lure to an addiction doesn't necessarily have to be pleasure. When most people start smoking, for example, they don't really like the taste; and one has to acquire a taste for beer and coffee. In laboratory experiments, rats and monkeys have actually become addicted to painful electric shocks. At first the animals tried hard to avoid the shocks, but after being exposed to them regularly, the animals came

14

to expect the pain and sought it out when it was not delivered on time. It seems that *any* stimulus can be addictive.

Perhaps it is the intensity of the experience that causes a person (or animal) to become hooked. Intense experiences, whether good or bad, can cause the body to react in ways that mild experiences cannot. (This theory might explain the addiction of people who compulsively take risks, even endangering their lives.) Or perhaps it is the frequency of an experience. Many indoctrination procedures are successful because the information is told over and over again, and eventually the person may start to believe it.

Because addictions usually run in cycles of pleasure followed by pain, researchers are looking at both ends of the cycle in their efforts to find causes and cures.

What Causes Addiction?

Why do some people become addicted to a particular substance or activity while others do not? More and more research is being conducted on the growing problem of addiction. So far, though, no one answer has been found to explain why some people become addicts or to predict who will be most at risk. In 1980, the National Institute of Drug Abuse (NIDA) published a description of forty-three possible theories to explain drug abuse.

Some researchers believe that anyone can become addicted. They say that anyone who takes an addictive substance over a long period of time will eventually become addicted.

Others feel that certain people are born with a predisposition to addiction. The children of alcoholics and overeaters, for example, are much more likely to follow in their parents' footsteps than children of parents who do not have these problems. There is some evidence that this predisposition is at least partially hereditary, not merely a set of learned behavior patterns.

And then there are those who believe addiction is a psychological problem. Researchers have been trying to find common denominators among

15

those who become addicted—to outline the "addictive personality." One common element found in nearly all addicts is low self-esteem. The development of a poor self-image may cause some people to become psychological dependents, people who seek out various crutches in life to compensate for their feelings of inadequacy. They are prime targets for addictions. In line with this theory, other studies have found stress and depression as major factors leading to addictions.

Other typical characteristics are impulsiveness, a need for instant gratification, and a feeling of social alienation. People who turn to drugs or other addictions are generally unable to cope with life's disappointments. Some psychologists believe that this inability to cope arises in people who were neglected or overprotected in their early years. Children who are constantly criticized may turn to addictive substances as a way of subconsciously punishing themselves.

To these types of people, addictive substances offer an appealing crutch whenever stress or disappointments arise. They give the user a false sense of power and security. Then a vicious circle begins, in which the person feels that security and power can be found only by using that addictive substance.

Some researchers believe that some types of people have a constant need for new sensations and experiences. When life seems dull and monotonous, they turn to addictive substances or activities to add excitement or new stimuli. Another theory contends that some people are unable to experience pleasure, except through the highs produced by addictive substances and activities.

Psychiatrist Edward Khantzian of Harvard Medical School believes that the main motivation for drug use is to relieve pain and escape—at least temporarily—from problems. He finds that people seem instinctively to choose the kind of drug that relieves their particular problems. Violent, aggressive people tend to choose narcotics that dull their emotions and make them feel "mellow." People who find it difficult to show their feelings often

16

turn to alcohol for its ability to remove inhibitions. People who are feeling low may take cocaine to give them feelings of power and energy. In each case, it seems that the addict is trying unconsciously to self-medicate, using a drug to treat a mood or personality problem.

Most addicts first use addictive substances for social reasons. Their friends are doing it, and so they do, too. Usually the first time someone offers it to them they refuse, but after a while they give in to peer pressure. Family situation also has a lot to do with addiction. Children whose parents are substance abusers are more likely to be substance abusers themselves. Sometimes children of addicts will avoid the particular substance their parents use but become addicted to something else instead. For example, a teenage girl with an alcoholic parent may become food obsessed and become anorexic or bulimic.

Some adolescents abuse drugs and other addictive substances as a form of rebellion against their parents and society. Mixed messages from the media may prompt some young people to try illegal and other addictive substances. Each day TV programs, movies, and popular songs bombard us with the message that it's "cool" to smoke, drink, and do drugs.

Why does a person with an addictive personality choose a particular substance or activity over another? A number of factors come into play in the "choice of poison," including personality, character, amount of money, life-style, and social customs, but most of all availability. Cocaine, for example, was at one time a "yuppie" drug, taken mainly by the affluent, while heroin was the drug most used in slum areas. Now that cocaine is widely available in forms like crack that are sold in small, relatively inexpensive amounts, the cocaine epidemic is spreading explosively. Crack is rapidly displacing heroin in the city slums and is also being tried by growing numbers of young people everywhere.

Although there are many exceptions, a person's particular type of addiction is often related to gender. Most compulsive gamblers and

17

alcoholics are men. More women are addicted to tranquilizers and sleeping pills. Generally, men are more likely to become addicted to aggressive outgoing activities, while women are more susceptible to passive or secretive activities. Of course, this pattern is changing in today's society, where women are taking on many roles that were traditionally male.

There is not really a conflict among the numerous theories on why people become addicted. Many researchers believe addiction is determined by a combination of factors, including environment, genetic, psychological, and biological influences.

The Addiction Problem

Addiction is a serious problem in our world. There are more than ten million alcoholics in the United States alone, and two million cocaine addicts. Each year almost a third of a million Americans die because of tobacco use, and 100,000 die because of alcohol. Overeating is a serious problem: up to one in three Americans is overweight, and obesity has been shown to be linked with increased health problems. Millions of people find their lives being controlled by various compulsions, from television watching, to gambling, to working too hard. Even hobbies can become self-destructive when they begin to interfere with our lives and our interactions with others. Valuable life experiences are being lost to addictions.

The destructive effects of addictive behavior are not limited to the addicts themselves. The lives of family members are disrupted by the addict's erratic and self-centered actions. Members of the community may suffer, too. Crime rates have skyrocketed in recent years, and many believe the increase is linked to drug addiction. Drug use on the job adds to the accident toll and saps our productivity; on the highways both alcohol and other addictive drugs can result in fatal mistakes. Now health officials have another reason to worry about drug addiction. Drug addicts are one of the highest risk groups for AIDS and are helping to spread the disease to the general public.

Eventually most people with an addiction problem find their lives in such a tangled mess that they seek help to try to "kick the habit." But kicking the habit doesn't mean the addict's problems are over. Most drug treatment experts believe "once an addict, always an addict." The addiction will never be cured, but it can be controlled, even for a person's whole life.

Beginning in the 1980s, the American public became increasingly aware of the problems addiction brings. "Say No to Drugs" is one of the most well-known expressions in the country. "Drug Free School Zone" signs can be found all across the country. Drug, alcohol, and smoking treatment programs are being filled to capacity. Self-help groups have sprung up everywhere for people addicted to everything from shopping, to love, to gambling, to television watching.

With all the current awareness of addiction problems, there still is no general agreement on how best to combat them. Indeed, society's attitudes are confusing and contradictory. Alcoholism, for example, is regarded as a disease by the American Medical Association, Alcoholics Anonymous, the National Council on Alcoholism, the National Institute on Alcohol Abuse and Alcoholism, and many other groups and organizations. Yet in 1988, the Supreme Court ruled that alcoholics are responsible for their condition—that alcoholism cannot be considered a handicap, but rather an act of "willful misconduct." The decision pertained specifically to educational benefits that two veterans were trying to have extended because their alcoholism had prevented them from pursuing their education within the period of eligibility. The court said, "It is not our role to resolve this medical issue on which the authorities remain sharply divided." Many experts are concerned about what this decision will mean for the treatment of alcoholism. Many insurance companies currently cover some of the costs of treatment programs because alcoholism was considered an addictive disease. Will the Supreme Court's decision affect the coverage?

The implication of this controversy are actually far broader. Both the experts and the general public are still sharply divided on the question of whether alcoholism and other addictions should be considered a disease with a physical basis (perhaps in the brain's biochemistry) or as the consequence of choices a person makes, consciously or unconsciously. Is an addict helpless against the force of the addiction?

Some experts say the idea of addiction as an illness helps addicts to overcome their problem—they realize that they are not morally bad or mentally ill, but have a physical illness that can be treated. Others object that the disease concept hinders the prevention of addiction: the average person may feel that he or she does not have the "addictive disease" and so can experiment with alcohol and drugs without any lasting harm.

Another serious reservation is prompted by the question of responsibility for actions committed by an addict under the influence of a drug. If addicts are viewed as victims of a disease, then they are not fully in control of their actions. Yet, what if someone commits murder while under the influence of a drug to which he or she is addicted? This is not just a hypothetical question. In 1989, a jury decided not to declare New York lawyer Joel Steinberg guilty of murder in the death of his young daughter Lisa because he was a habitual drug user and was under the influence of cocaine at the time of the fatal beating. In cases like that, addiction has become the ultimate cop-out.

The laws governing the most common addictive substances are also a maze of contradictory policies and mixed signals. Drugs such as cocaine and heroin are illegal; so is marijuana. But cigarettes and alcohol, each of which kills more people than all illegal drugs combined, can be legally sold and used, although they are age restricted. Since 1966, federal laws requires a health warning on cigarette cartons (while the same federal government subsidizes tobacco growers), but similar warning labels were not required on alcoholic beverages until 1989. Cigarette commercials are banned from television, but beer, wine, and wine cooler advertisements are growing in number. (The average child will see 10,000 beer commercials before his or her eighteenth birthday!) Many states require insurance companies to cover alcohol and drug treatment programs, but no laws require coverage of programs to stop smoking.

Meanwhile, scientists are exploring all aspects of the addiction problem, hoping that increased understanding will lead to solutions. In this book we'll explore the state of current knowledge regarding the various kinds of addictions and the progress toward conquering them. First, though, we need to take a closer look at the brain. Here, in its microscopic structures and chemical interactions, researchers are gaining the most promising insights into the causes and control of addiction.

The authors consulted hundreds of books, articles, and pamphlets—some of them extremely technical—in writing this book. The references listed here and at the ends of later chapters represent a selection of the more readily available ones that may be useful for readers who would like more information in particular areas. Addresses of sources of information and help are also provided.

Further Reading

Berger, Gilda. *Addiction: Its Causes, Problems, and Treatments.* New York: Franklin Watts, 1982.

Hodgkinson, Liz. *Addictions: What They Are—Why They Happen—How to Help.* Wellingborough, England: Thorsons Publishing Group, 1986.

Hurley, Dan. "Cycles of Craving." *Psychology Today,* July/August, 1989, pp. 54–58.

Peele, Stanton. "Ain't Misbehavin': Addiction Has Become an All-Purpose Excuse." *The Sciences,* July/August, 1989, pp. 14–21.

Drugs and the Brain

"Tell me where is fancy bred,
Or in the heart, or in the head?"

Shakespeare was far ahead of his time even to consider the head as the source of the tender emotions of love. In his day and, indeed, for several centuries afterward, most people were convinced that the heart was the source of emotions. The head was regarded as the center of rational thought—the opposite of the often illogical emotions.

Now we know that the heart, although vital, is only the pump that supplies the organs of the body with blood. It is influenced by emotions, but they are generated in the brain.

The Brain

It seems amazing that thoughts, memories, emotions, dreams—all the unique characteristics that make up an individual personality—have their origin in the three-pound jellylike mass of the brain. This remarkable organ controls all the workings of the body as well: heartbeat, breathing, walking, talking—all of our conscious and unconscious actions.

Researchers have used a variety of techniques to learn about the brain and its functions. Tiny electrical impulses, picked up at the surface of the face and scalp, provide clues to the activity inside the brain. Sophisticated scanners can survey the brain's inner structures without harming them; some can also pinpoint the precise parts of the brain that are active during various activities.

By stimulating different parts of the brain (sometimes with electrodes or probes so fine that they act on just a single nerve cell), researchers have been able to draw up maps of brain functions. On the surface, they have found areas that receive the messages of the senses, other areas that control the movement of body parts, and still other regions that are involved in under-standing and producing speech, in decision making, and in various aspects of personality. Deep within the brain, scientists have found key centers that control breathing and heartbeat; centers that govern appetites for food, water, and sex; and a number of structures involved in the emotions of fear, rage, and pleasure.

The working parts of the brain are rather simple structures: the individual nerve cells or *neurons*. Each neuron acts like a tiny switch that can be either on or off. The brain is able to store huge amounts of information and control and coordinate many varied and complicated functions because it has huge numbers of neurons—tens of billions of them—all interconnected into a complex tangle of branching pathways.

Neurons and Neurotransmitters

The neuron is a microscopic structure composed of three main parts: the cell body or *soma;* the *axon,* which looks like a long thread with a raveled end and carries signals away from the cell body; and the branching *dendrites,* which receive stimuli from neighboring nerve cells.

Like a switch, the soma can be on or off, depending on the signals it receives from its neighboring nerve cells. If a strong enough "on" message comes in, the soma "fires," sending an impulse to the axon. The impulse is carried along the axon by a series of electrochemical reactions, and it travels much more slowly than the electrical impulses that speed along a telephone

24

wire. Each nerve impulse has the same strength. The frequency of the impulses (that is, the number that pass along the axon each second) is what determines how intense the message will be. The stab of a pinprick, for example, is much more intense than the tickle of an ant walking on your fingertip; this intensity is determined by the frequency of the nerve message.

In the intricate networks of the brain, the individual neurons in a particular sequence are not actually connected to each other. Instead, they are separated by a tiny gap called a *synapse*. On one side of the synapse (the presynaptic side) is a nerve ending from the long fibrous axon. On the other (the postsynaptic side) are the dendrites of another nerve cell. The message is carried across the synapse by molecules of chemicals called *neurotransmitters*. These chemical messengers are stored in the endings of the axon in tiny structures called *vesicles*. When a neuron fires, neurotransmitters are released and pour out into the synapse. They move slowly through the watery fluid that fills the gap and then are taken up by the endings of the dendrites on the other side. These neurotransmitters can attach only at specific sites designed just for them. The neurotransmitter is like a key that can open only the lock or *receptor* that has the correct shape.

If enough of the receptors in the dendrites of the next neuron have neurotransmitters attached to them, the electric charge of the dendrite membrane changes, and a series of electrochemical reactions travels along the dendrite, carrying the message on to the soma. Meanwhile, other impulses are coming in through other dendrites. Some of them may be "on" signals, prompting the soma to fire; but others, carried by different neurotransmitters or regulated by different kinds of receptors, may be "off" signals that stop or inhibit the nerve cell's action. The combination of impulses determines whether the soma will fire and transmit the message through its axon to other nerve cells.

The synapse thus provides a way of fine-tuning the flow of nerve impulses in the brain, stopping certain messages and strengthening others.

25

Dozens of neurotransmitters have already been discovered, and researchers believe there may ultimately turn out to be hundreds of them. The same neurotransmitter may have different effects on different types of neurons, stimulating some and inhibiting others, depending on the kind of receptor the nerve cell carries on its surface.

Normally the nerve cell receptors hold on to the neurotransmitters they captured for only a millisecond or two; then the electrical balance of the neuron is restored. As a result, the nerve message is sent only once following a particular stimulus, not again and again. The neurotransmitters travel back into the synapse, where they are either broken down by enzymes (biochemicals that help other chemicals to react) or are taken up again by the axon of the presynaptic neuron and stored in vesicles for reuse at a later time.

The brain thus works through a network of chemical and electrical reactions. The flow of electrochemical impulses makes it possible for us to think, speak, and move and controls the complex internal reactions that keep us alive.

Chemical Deceivers

Sometimes the nerve cells can be tricked. Drugs like cocaine, for example, can interfere with normal functioning of the brain's neurons. Cocaine works on a neurotransmitter called *dopamine,* which acts in certain areas of the brain to produce feelings of pleasure. The drug acts in three ways to increase the dopamine effects: it stimulates the neurons to release large amounts of dopamine into the synapses; it blocks the enzyme that normally stops dopamine's action on the nerve cell receptors; and it also blocks the reuptake of dopamine into the vesicles of the axons. As a result, the postsynaptic neuron continues to fire, producing a "rush" or "high." The cocaine user has a feeling of being "speeded up," and perceptions of the world are altered. But the axons of the presynaptic neurons have a shortage of dopamine, and it takes some time to produce more. As a result, the cocaine high is soon followed by a "crash." The flow of pleasurable feelings ebbs, and the person feels miserable.

Other drugs can slow down the flow of neurotransmitters to produce feelings of relaxation. Some chemicals have similar shapes and can attach to the wrong receptor sites. These wrong neurotransmitters do not affect the neuron's electrical balance and thus do not cause the cell to fire. But they are blocking the receptors, preventing the real neurotransmitters from reaching them. As a result, a message that would have been sent may not get through.

By the use of drugs or activities that speed up or slow down the transmission of neurochemicals, people can alter their mood and the way they perceive the world. The enzymes that control the production and breakdown of neurotransmitters provide a built-in defense against this kind of biochemical tampering. When a person continually uses drugs or engages in activities that slow down or speed up the flow of nerve messages, the brain compensates by changing the level of key enzymes. If the neurons are firing too much, more of the enzymes that destroy neurotransmitters will be produced. If the neurons are not firing enough, more enzymes that create neurotransmitters will be made available. Thus, the body changes the amount of stimulation needed to create a response. When more than normal amounts of a neurotransmitter are flooding the neurons, the chemical may also stimulate the formation of additional receptors on the dendrite membranes; or it may activate enzymes that destroy some of the receptors and make the neuron less sensitive to the stimulus. In these ways, a person builds up tolerance toward the action of the substance or activity, and more is needed to create the same response.

Because the change in enzyme and receptor levels in the brain is such a slow and gradual process, it takes time to return to normal once it is changed. However, with the new enzyme balance, the brain cells have adapted to a new level of stimulation—they now need the drug or activity in order to work properly; without it, the person no longer feels normal. That is why a person experiences a "low" after the "high" of the addictive behavior passes—because the stimulation that slowed down or speeded up neurotransmission is gone, but the new level of stimulation is still needed for the neurons to fire. This enzyme imbalance may also cause other uncomfortable effects, which are referred to as withdrawal symptoms because they occur when the substance or activity is no longer stimulating the brain. The person takes another dose to try to relieve the symptoms. But each new dose just contributes further to the enzyme imbalance and makes things worse.

Pleasure

What kinds of things give you pleasure? Does your favorite song send tingles shivering down your spine? Does a bit of chocolate cake send a rush of good feelings through you?

What causes the feeling of pleasure? Scientists believe that pleasure is the result of chemical reactions in the brain that are stimulated by various events. They provide a positive reinforcement for certain activities, a reward that motivates us to do them again. Normally the kinds of actions that stimulate pleasure are positive ones for the body's health and survival (eating food and drinking fluids, for example) or the survival of the species (such as sexual activity and caring for babies). But humans can also learn new reactions, and harmful forms of behavior may become linked with pleasure responses. Mood-altering drugs can act at the source of pleasurable feelings, working on the brain's biochemistry.

James Olds, an American researcher at Canada's McGill University, accidentally discovered the brain's pleasure center. He was experimenting with rats, studying a part of the brain called the hypothalamus, which houses a number of important control centers. Olds had meant to place an electrode in the rat's hypothalamus, but his aim was a bit off—as he discovered when he sent a tiny electric current through the electrode. Stimulation of the hypothalamus normally produces discomfort. Olds had planned to stimulate the electrode whenever the rat went into a particular corner; he expected the rat to avoid that corner once it realized the connection. Instead of avoiding the corner, however, the rat kept going back again and again.

The McGill research team tried placing electrodes in the same part of other rats' brains. When they allowed the rats to stimulate the electrodes themselves, some of the rodents did so thousands of times in a row, until they collapsed in exhaustion. The rats chose the stimulation over eating, drinking, sleeping, and mating. Their reaction was similar to that found in many drug addicts.

It wasn't long before others realized the importance of the discovery of the brain as the source of pleasure. Scientists began studying the chemical reactions that take place in the brain, suspecting that the actions of neurotransmitters were responsible for all of the emotions we experience. In 1973, a twenty-six-year-old graduate student, Candace Pert, working with Solomon Snyder at Johns Hopkins University, discovered the "keyhole" or receptor for opiates such as morphine and heroin.

Researchers wondered why brain cells should contain receptors that seemed tailor-made for a foreign substance—a chemical found solely in a poppy plant that grows naturally only in a small region of the world. Perhaps there was some sort of opiatelike substance in the brain, they thought, one that would have effects similar to those of the morphine drugs. In 1974, John Hughes and Hans Kosterlitz of the University of Aberdeen, Scotland, discovered some of those natural opiates—brain chemicals that fit precisely into the opiate receptors. The researchers named these new compounds *endorphins*, short for "endogenous morphines." (Endogenous means produced inside.)

In 1980, at the Addiction Research Laboratory at Stanford University, another important step in studying the biochemistry of pleasure was taken. Neuroscientist Avram Goldstein had student volunteers listen to their favorite music in a soundproof booth. Whenever the students felt a shiver of pleasure, they raised their hands. Then some of the students were given an injection of a drug called naloxone. The volunteers who had received the injection raised their hands much less than they did before, and much less than the others who received a placebo injection (an injection that had no drugs in it). Naloxone works by blocking endorphins, so it seemed apparent that endorphins are produced whenever we experience pleasure.

Research into the biochemistry of the brain expanded rapidly after that. Researchers began to explore the activities of the brain's neurotransmitters, and endorphins in particular. Soon they were claiming that endorphins were involved in practically everything we experience from birth to death.

Endorphins

Studies and speculations have already implicated endorphins in a virtually endless list of behaviors and experiences. They range from compulsive eating to compulsive gambling, from laughing to crying, from stress to the body's immune system. Endorphins have been linked to near-death experiences, pregnancy, and birth. They are triggered by the trauma of injury and enhance the satisfaction of petting one's dog, as well as eating chocolates or hot chili peppers; their secretion is also stimulated by undergoing acupuncture and massage, listening to music, performing strenuous aerobic exercises, and meditating.

Endorphins or their opiate receptors have been found nearly everywhere in the body—in the brain, in the bloodstream, in the heart and lungs, and in the digestive, reproductive, and endocrine systems. However, researchers are still not totally sure exactly what role endorphins play. They seem to have an important part in keeping the body running smoothly, but not a life-and-death role. People who receive injections of drugs that block opiates do not stop breathing, and their hearts don't stop, but they do feel more pain and experience less of a "high" from normally endorphin-producing activities.

It seems that the pleasure-producing effects of the endorphin response provide rewards that reinforce health-promoting activities. They are also involved in the body's natural relief from pain. Often an injury—even a broken bone—doesn't seem to hurt very much at first. The severe pain is not felt until a while after the injury. Endorphin levels rise after an injury, deadening the pain as a natural survival mechanism, enabling us to flee from the danger that may have caused the injury.

Endorphin levels also rise continuously during pregnancy and reach a peak just before and during labor. Then, after helping the woman cope with the pain of giving birth, they drop dramatically within twenty-four hours after delivery. Perhaps this drop in endorphin levels is responsible for the postpartum depression that many women experience after the birth of a child.

Acupuncture is thought to ease pain by causing the release of endorphins. (The pain-relieving effect is blocked if the person is given an injection of naloxone.) Placebos seem to work in a similar way. In one study, some patients gained the same pain relief from a shot that they *thought* was a drug as they did from a mild dose of morphine. The patient's belief that a treatment can help relieve pain is all that is needed to produce the effect. (The placebo effect, too, is blocked by naloxone.)

Some researchers believe that people can even become addicted to pain! After an experience with the flood of endorphins that follows an injury, there may be an unconscious motivation to repeat the experience—by self-inflicted injuries, if necessary. This theory may explain why autistic children self-destructively bang their heads or hurt other parts of their bodies. Researchers at the New England Medical Center in Boston are exploring this idea by setting up an exercise program for autistic children, to allow an alternative means of endorphin production.

According to Theodore Cicero at Washington University Medical School, endorphins play "probably the dominant role in regulating reproductive hormone cycles." Researchers had suspected a link between endorphins and sex because of the fact that many heroin and morphine users often display a lack of desire for sex. This finding suggested that the body's natural opiates may suppress the sex drive. The hindrance may have arisen in the body so that reproduction would occur when things were going well and not during troubled times. The Washington University team also noted that the maturing of the body's system of natural opiates seems to parallel the maturation of the reproductive system. When young rats are given opiates, they mature much later than normal; but when they receive opiate blockers, they mature more quickly. This fact has sobering implications for young people who take drugs. They could be delaying their maturation or even sacrificing their future choice of having children.

Other studies have found endorphins to be involved in laughter. Laughter lessens depression, fear, anger, and other damaging emotions, and endorphins are thought to be behind this effect. Tears have been found to contain leucine-enkephalin—an endorphin! Just what role it plays in tears is not known for sure, but crying helps relieve stress.

A number of studies have implicated endorphins in various eating disorders, and some researchers believe they are behind all addictive behaviors.

Not all scientists are convinced about endorphins, though. Some feel too much is being credited to the neurochemical. They point to the fact that although elevated levels of endorphins have been shown in the blood of people who run, for example, their presence there does not necessarily mean that the brain experiences increased levels of endorphins as well. Still, the debate goes on as research into the workings of these neurochemicals continues to bring new insights into the normal functions of the brain and the changes that occur in addiction.

The more we learn about the brain's role in pleasure, the more questions arise. Why, for example, do some people find pleasure in experiences that cause fear in others? It is a basic goal of all creatures to avoid pain and seek pleasurable experiences. Brain researchers hope that the knowledge they are gaining will bring cures for sadness, anxiety, and depression and help us to discover why we do the things we do.

Further Reading

Barnes, Deborah M. "Meeting on the Mind." *Science*, January 8, 1988, pp. 142-144.

"Freedom from Addictions." *Prevention Health Series*, 1984, pp. 155–163.

Hooper, Judith. "The Brain's River of Rewards." *American Health*, December 1987, pp. 37–41.

Hopson, Janet L. "A Pleasurable Chemistry." *Psychology Today*, July/August 1988, pp. 29–33.

Levinthal, Charles F. *Messengers of Paradise: Opiates and the Brain*. New York: Anchor Press, 1988.

Milkman, Harvey and Stanley Sunderwirth. *Craving for Ecstasy: The Consciousness & Chemistry of Escape*. Lexington, Mass.: D. C. Heath & Co., 1987.

Pennisi, Elizabeth. "Addiction and the Brain." *Science Year 1988*. Chicago: World Book, pp. 117-127.

Rapoport, J.L. "The Biology of Obsessions and Compulsions." *Scientific American*, March 1989, pp. 82–89.

Restak, Richard M., MD. *The Mind*. New York: Bantam, 1988.

Siegel, Ronald K., PhD. *Intoxication: Life in Pursuit of Artificial Paradise*. New York: EP Dutton, 1989.

Snyder, Solomon H. *Brainstorming: The Science and Politics of Opiate Research*. Cambridge, Mass.: Harvard University Press, 1989.

For More Information

Addiction Research Foundation
33 Russell Street
Toronto, Canada M5S 2S1

Substance Addictions

In a recent nationwide poll, close to half the people interviewed named drugs as America's most serious problem. Three out of four said we should spend more money on the government's anti-drug programs.

Alcohol, nicotine, and caffeine are all drugs, but these are not the drugs most people are concerned about now. For the average person, "drug addiction" calls to mind cocaine, heroin, and marijuana. These drugs—and most others that are abused—are illegal drugs. According to the United States Food and Drug Administration (FDA), a drug abuser "deliberately takes a substance for other than its intended purpose, and in a manner that can result in damage to the person's health or his ability to function." Even legal drugs can be abused, and then their abuse becomes illegal. Not all drug abusers are addicted, but continued abuse of addictive drugs usually leads to addiction eventually.

Drug abuse and drug addiction are serious health problems for most of the world. Drug use can cause physical damage to the user's body (often permanent damage), and an overdose can be deadly. Moreover, a drug user may suffer from mental confusion, impaired judgment, and a loss of physical coordination and of the ability to react quickly to demanding situations. Many drug abusers are unable to carry on normal lives, going to school or keeping a job. Yet a drug habit can be very expensive. The drug abuser may turn to crime to satisfy the often painful cravings for drugs.

35

Americans spend more than $100 billion each year on illegal drugs. The government spends over $10 billion to try to stop drugs from entering the country and being sold. But only 5 to 10 percent of all the illegal drugs are confiscated.

Many people experiment with drugs. In 1987, it was estimated that seventy million Americans had tried an illegal drug—that's more than one out of three people! (Twenty-five years ago, only one in twenty-five had used an illegal drug.) Fortunately, most people who try drugs don't get hooked and never try them again. Of the twenty to thirty million who have tried cocaine, for example, less than six million are regular users. Most of the seventy million who have experimented with drugs have tried marijuana, but less than one in four still use it on a regular basis. Although it is encouraging that drug use doesn't necessarily mean the user will be hooked for life, the numbers of users and abusers are shocking.

Perhaps the most shocking fact about drug abuse is the age at which it starts. Between 50 and 65 percent of all high school students will have used an illegal drug before they graduate. The average age a child first uses drugs is thirteen years old, and a *Weekly Reader* poll found that one out of three nine-year-olds feels pressure to try drugs! Facts like these have alarmed the parents of the nation, and the U.S. government declared an all-out war against drugs in 1986.

History of Addictive Drugs

Most addictive drugs reduce pain and were originally used as medicines. Morphine, opium, cocaine, heroin, amphetamines, barbiturates, and tranquilizers were all designed for medicinal purposes. However, doctors noticed that many became addicted to these drugs.

We tend to think of drug abuse as a new problem, but actually it has a long history in this country. In the late 1700s, alcohol abuse was the main concern, and a federal law was passed to ration the amount of liquor allowed for soldiers. In the mid-1800s, opium abuse began to spread. At this time, new advances in technology were resulting in changing values and social upheaval. Life became more complicated and more stress-filled as people came to the cities to work, and opiate drugs were seen as a way to cope with these new problems. Cocaine was a widely used "wonder drug" and even (from 1886 to 1903) an ingredient in a popular beverage, Coca-Cola. Shortly after the turn of the century, a *New York Times* report claimed there were one and a half million American drug users.

The federal government tried desperately to stop this growing drug problem, first with the Pure Food and Drug Act in 1906 and then, in 1914, with the Harrison Act, which labeled all drugs that were sold without a prescription illegal.

The second great outbreak of drug use in the United States was in the 1960s, when the nation's youth turned to drugs in rebellion against a government they felt was pushing the country into an unjust war in Vietnam. Marijuana, LSD, and heroin were drugs of choice at that time. But drug abuse was not confined to the young. Many adults were hooked on prescribed tranquilizers to help them cope with the stresses of daily life, and amphetamines to counteract the negative side effects of the tranquilizers.

The deaths of rock superstars like Jim Morrison, Jimi Hendrix, and Janis Joplin helped to take some of the glamour away from "hard drugs," and heroin and LSD gradually went out of favor. But marijuana use remained widespread in the 1970s, with many people considering it "as harmless as alcohol."

By the 1980s, cocaine had become the fashionable drug of abuse. For the average person, though, legal drugs like alcohol and tobacco were still the overwhelming favorites. In a 1987 poll, 86 percent of the high school students interviewed said they used alcohol (although virtually all of them were under the legal drinking age). Except for cocaine, the use of illegal drugs by young people has been dropping in recent years.

Stages of Drug Abuse

According to experts such as Ken Barun, a drug abuse counselor who works with young people, drug abusers usually go through progressive stages. The amount of time it takes for drug abuse to progress varies widely, from a few months to several years.

Experimental stage. Most who experiment with tobacco, alcohol, and marijuana eventually give them up. Peer pressure motivates them to experiment with these gateway drugs. Experimenting adolescents learn that drugs can alter a person's moods, but drug use is not a significant part of their lives.

Casual stage. In the second stage of drug abuse, the drug user takes drugs more often but believes he or she can quit anytime. The person who has progressed to this stage might try drugs like uppers and downers in addition to gateway drugs.

Progressive stage. In the third stage of drug abuse, the drug user seeks out drugs to change his or her moods, believing they are the only way of finding pleasure. Mood swings from extreme highs to extreme lows are common. Drug use has progressed to other types such as cocaine and hallucinogenic drugs. Although the person will deny that any problem exists, his or her body has built up a tolerance toward certain drugs, as well as a physical dependency.

Terminal stage. In the final stage of drug abuse, the user feels he or she cannot live without drugs and is dependent on them just to feel normal. Heroin and other opiates are used in this stage, as well as any number of other drugs. The life of a drug abuser in the terminal stage is a shambles. He or she cannot hold down a job or remain in school and can think of nothing but getting high.

Profile of a Drug Addict

Drug abusers seem to have many characteristics in common. Often they do not do well in school, and they tend to have a negative attitude toward authority. They have low self-esteem and are typically loners—alienated from family and friends. The often have difficulty in expressing themselves. They may be anxious and depressed quite often and are unable to deal with frustration, problems, and disappointments. They expect a lot but don't expect to work hard for what they want. These characteristics are especially typical of those whose drug problems begin at an early age, but they apply to adult drug abusers as well.

The typical addict's family life has similar characteristics as well. Often parents are separated or divorced, abuse their children, or are drug users or alcoholics themselves. Sometimes the parents are quite the opposite of abusive, but are overprotective. There is usually very little communication between parents and children, and if there are rules concerning proper behavior, they are rarely enforced.

Most parents are worried about drugs affecting their kids, but few realize it when their own children are involved. Various studies have found that only one-quarter to one-half of parents of drug users realize their kids use drugs. At a study in one school district, 80 percent of the parents thought that marijuana was a problem for students in their district, but only 20 percent thought their children were users. Actually, 33 percent of the children were regular pot smokers, and over half had tried marijuana.

Concerned parents and friends can look for various signs that might suggest someone is using drugs. The most obvious is finding drugs, or drug paraphernalia. But there are many behavioral changes that might indicate a drug problem as well. These include:

1. extreme mood changes
2. secretive behavior
3. irresponsibility at school or work and at home
4. lack of ambition
5. changes in friends and hangouts
6. sudden sloppy dressing
7. deteriorating health

In other words, any sudden sharp change in behavior may be a warning of a serious problem.

Drug Use Among Adolescents

Although cigarettes, alcohol, and marijuana are gateway drugs, not everyone who tries them will go on to harder drugs. If a dependency on one of these develops, though, chances are greater that other drug dependencies will arise.

Dr. Robert L. DuPont, Jr., former White House drug chief, declared: "The earlier in life a child starts using any dependence-producing drug, the more likely he or she is to experience dependence and other health problems and go on to other dependence-producing drugs."

Twelve to seventeen-year-olds who smoke cigarettes are twice as likely to use alcohol, ten times more likely to smoke marijuana, and fourteen times more likely to use cocaine and heroin than twelve- to seventeen-year-olds who don't smoke.

In one study, one-quarter of those who had tried marijuana also tried cocaine, hallucinogens, and opiates; and 93 percent of all cocaine users have tried marijuana. Statistics like these have led many to believe in the "stepping stone" theory of drug progression. Although trying "lesser" drugs like marijuana does not necessarily lead to trying and becoming hooked on others, a person's chances of never getting hooked are a lot better if he or she never tries them. Once an adolescent hangs around with friends who smoke marijuana, it is only a matter of time before one member of the group decides to try something else, and that something else then becomes a thing for the rest of the group to try as well.

When do kids start taking drugs? The average age of first drug use is thirteen years old. According to NIDA, the average age for first trying various drugs is:

> Age 17   for cocaine
>
> Age 16   for LSD, PCP, amyl and butyl nitrate

Age 15   for heroin and tranquilizers

Age 14   for tobacco, alcohol, marijuana, barbiturates,

Quaaludes, stimulants, and sedatives

Ages 12 to 13   for inhalants (glue sniffing)

Why kids use drugs. Most people think that teenagers are lured into drugs by pushers lurking outside the schoolyard. Actually, however, kids' attitudes toward drugs are largely shaped by their parents' attitudes toward drugs. Even more important than the things parents say is the way they act about drugs—not just illegal drugs but all kinds. According to the Pacific Institute for Research and Evaluation, children are more likely to abuse drugs when their parents:

1.   abuse alcohol

2.   smoke cigarettes

3.   take illegal drugs

4.   take any kind of drug to relieve stress or emotional worries

5.   are very strongly for or against drugs

There are many reasons why a young person might begin taking drugs. In one California study, adolescents said they used drugs because they wanted to escape problems, because their friends use drugs, because drugs make them feel good, because they wanted to experiment, and because they were bored. In addition to these reasons there are many underlying factors, like society's mixed messages, conflicts that arise due to physical or hormonal changes that occur during adolescence, the desire to be independent or feel grown-up, low self-esteem, stress caused by family problems, and depression caused by any of these or other problems.

Our society gives mixed messages about drugs. On the one hand, kids are told "Drugs are bad. Say no to drugs." But our culture also tends to glorify drug use. Many abusers are public heroes in sports, music, and entertainment—heroes that kids look up to and want to be like. Taking substances to relieve physical and psychological problems is an accepted and ingrained behavior for modern people. The fact that some mood-altering substances are legal and others are not may seem strange and arbitrary.

Adolescents go through many changes as their bodies develop into adults. They are caught between the world of the adult and the world of the child—not quite either. The world won't see them as adults, but they don't feel like children anymore. They want to be independent, but they still need the security of the family. They are searching for their own individuality, but they need desperately to feel they belong, and they feel an enormous pressure to be like their friends.

For many young people, smoking cigarettes is a way of feeling grown up. But tobacco can be a gateway to other drugs. Not all kids who smoke cigarettes will necessarily try other drugs, but smoking greatly increases their chances.

Low self-esteem is one of the major characteristics of drug users. People who don't think much of themselves are often more vulnerable to peer pressure because they want desperately to be accepted and to belong. Family problems can contribute greatly to insecurities in young people that could lead them to seek refuge in drugs. Today four out of ten children's parents are divorced, and one in twelve kids is raised by a single parent. Families move more often, and kids may have to make new friends many times. More than half of all mothers work, and children spend less time with their families than ever before. One study found that the number one factor in common for children with problems in school was being left on their own after school. According to another study, average parents interact with their kids for less than fifteen minutes a day! A University of Michigan Institute for Social Research study found that students who did not spend much time at home were more likely to abuse drugs.

Many scientists believe there is a strong link between depression and addictive behavior. Drug addiction in adolescents is no exception. According to a *Newsweek* cover story, 400,000 seven- to twelve-year-olds experience depression. Young people often react to depression by engaging in self-destructive behavior such as delinquency, promiscuity, and drug or alcohol abuse.

Boredom is one reason kids say they use drugs. "There's nothing better to do." Some psychologists believe that television may be at least partly to blame. Children who grow up watching too much television have been found in some studies to have shorter attention spans and to become bored more easily. Some psychologists feel that because television watching is a passive activity, children who watch a lot of television as an escape from boredom may have a greater tendency to use drugs, which are all also a passive escape from boredom. Psychologists suggest that other alternatives besides television should be explored to prevent boredom. Exercise is ideal because it stimulates the mind and the body. Exercise also stimulates the production of the body's own natural drug, endorphins, and it can be learned as a positive way of feeling good without drugs. Group exercise also fosters interactive skills with other people, which helps prevent isolation and alienation—another common trait in drug abusers.

Prevention

Drugs do make kids feel better for the moment, and they seem to make problems temporarily go away. But they damage the body, and they can kill. Exercise, helping others, and striving for achievements all can make people feel good about themselves; they are constructive goals that help make life better for everyone. These are some of the basic ideas behind the 15,000 "Just Say No" clubs around the country. The clubs give kids from seven to fourteen a place to get together, to have fun and make friends, and to learn how to say no to drugs. The groups combine educational activities with recreation and community service. Since peer pressure is the main reason kids turn to drugs, the clubs try to encourage kids to reverse the idea that drugs are cool and realize that it's cool *not* to do drugs.

The "Just Say No" clubs have a three-step plan to turn down drugs when a friend offers them to you:

Step 1: Decide whether what your friend wants to do is OK or not. Will it get you in trouble? Will it make you feel bad about yourself?

Step 2: If it isn't OK, just say no.

Step 3: Use peer pressure reversal by suggesting something else to do instead. For example, saying, "No thanks, but I'm going to go swimming. Do you want to come too?"

Other helpful hints about how to say no are to point out the negative side of drugs. Change the subject or give the excuse that you can't because you're in training or need to concentrate for a big test. Try to ignore repeated requests. If the pressure gets to be too much, walk away. At parties where people are using drugs, hang around those who aren't using them—or leave.

Project LEAD, Youth to Youth, and Students Against Drunk Driving are other support groups for adolescents. DARE (Drug Abuse Resistance Education) is a sixteen-week program conducted by police officers for kindergarten-through-eighth-graders. The instructors focus on drug education, building self-esteem, and encouraging children to "dare to say no!"

Where Should Kids Learn about Drugs?

Because drugs are out there, it's important for kids to know about drugs so that they can make intelligent decisions about them. Since kids start taking drugs at such an early age, some believe that they should learn about drugs as soon as possible—even as early as five or six!

Some feel that it is the parents' responsibility to teach their children about drugs. Others say that parents might not feel qualified and that the best place should be in school, by a qualified teacher. A survey of eleventh grade California students found that 59 percent learned about drugs in a class in school, and 66 percent learned about drugs from their friends. Only 29 percent of the teens polled learned about drugs from their parents, and 38 percent learned by trying drugs themselves.

In the past, drug education in school was not very effective; for one thing, it usually didn't start until high school, and by then it was too late. Information about drugs was given to students, but attitudes toward drugs weren't usually discussed. In addition, drug education said drugs were bad, but it didn't discuss how many people find temporary pleasure in them. To the adolescents who had already tried drugs, this omission didn't lend much credibility. A 1980 study of drug education courses around the country found that the classes were having very little effect on adolescent attitudes toward drugs.

However, things are changing. In recent studies more than 90 percent of the students felt that drug education had influenced their attitudes and behavior toward drugs. Indeed, there has been a dramatic increase in awareness of the dangers of drugs and a decrease in the use of drugs like marijuana over the last fifteen years.

Many teens get turned off when they hear "Just Say No," but many listen when their heroes tell them not to do drugs. Some of the biggest rock stars, like Bon Jovi, Mötley Crüe, and Bruce Hornsby, have made TV commercials against drugs as part of an ongoing campaign for Rock Against Drugs (RAD). Stars of popular television programs, like Michael J. Fox and Kirk Cameron, have made commercials that reach out to their audiences. For many kids, these idols are the only people they listen to, and the programs have met with enormous success.

Many who are against the "Just Say No" program started by former First Lady Nancy Reagan feel that it is condescending to adolescents. It does not deal with the underlying reasons behind why kids say yes—like low self-esteem. When kids are told drugs are bad and they don't seem to fit in with others, one outcome is that they'll try to fit in with the "bad."

Those against the "Just Say No" approach believe the government's attitude is too simplistic. The government believes we should cut the demand for drugs by punishing users. Some believe that only when we teach pride and help the youth of America build a positive self-image through parental support, encouragement by teachers and guidance counselors, and rehabilitation centers will educating kids about drugs succeed.

The Drug War

The drug problem is the number one concern of many Americans. The increase in crime and violence that goes along with drugs has everyone upset. The government spends billions each year fighting drug traffic and educating the public. Drug laws have gotten tougher. In 1986, a federal law banned all analogs of controlled substances (that is, chemically related compounds with similar effects). No longer should underground chemists sell "legal" designer drugs.

Citizens are taking the drug war into their own hands as well. Vigilante groups have sprung up, and neighborhood protection groups have been formed. In 1988 two Detroit residents were arrested for burning down a crack house—the neighbors had chipped in to buy the gasoline.

But still drug-related crimes increase. Fifty-five percent of all the murders committed in Los Angeles in 1987 were drug-related. The same is true for most major American cities. And it's only getting worse. In Washington, D.C., 17 percent of the homicides in 1985 were drug-related. In 1986 the number rose to 33 percent, in 1987 to 57 percent, and in 1988 to 67 percent. Often innocent bystanders are killed during drug gang wars. Even police have become the targets of drug pushers' bullets, as in the 1988 assassination of New York police officer Edward Byrne while he was protecting a citizen who had complained about drugs in his neighborhood. An undercover policeman in a Texas high school was murdered by a student drug dealer.

While former president Ronald Reagan was in office, his wife Nancy was a leading voice in the war against drugs. In outrage against the increasing violence that accompanies drug selling in America, Mrs. Reagan took a hard line against even casual drug users. "I'm saying that if you're a casual user, you're an accomplice to murder."

The drug concern has infiltrated all walks of life. A number of companies now require drug tests before hiring an employee, and many require random drug testing of current employees. Many people are upset about this practice, feeling it is an infringement of their rights. Drug tests are even available for parents to use on their children.

The all-out war on drugs has caused some problems for enforcement officials. Even with the limited funds and manpower available, there has been a dramatic increase in the number of drug-related arrests. In Detroit, for example, they have tripled. But prisons are getting more and more crowded. What do we do with all the offenders? The government believes that an education program to keep kids from turning to drugs is an important part of the answer.

Many law enforcement officials believe that an education program focused on just saying no is not enough. For inner-city kids who have little hope of getting the better things out of life, drug dealing is an attractive proposition. Drug running and drug dealing can bring in up to $2,000 a day for these ghetto kids. When they show up in school in expensive clothes and flaunt high-cost cars and gadgets, they're telling everyone that they are successful. No amount of education will make them believe that life can be better without drugs.

Some people say we are taking the wrong approach to the war on drugs. They believe drug use should be legalized. The supporters of legislation point to the experience of the late 1800s. At that time addiction was treated by doctors, not regulated by police. It was when people who used drugs became criminals that drug addiction grew in this country. In Great Britain today, heroin addicts can register with the government and receive legal supplies of the drug.

During prohibition in the 1920s and early 1930s, alcohol was an illegal drug in the United States, and its supply and sale financed an explosion of organized criminal activity. Now that alcohol is legal and readily available, there is no crime or violence associated with buying and selling liquor. The same would be true of drugs like marijuana, cocaine, and heroin, claim the supporters of legalization. If drugs were legal, then they would become cheaper, and users would not resort to crime to buy them. Drugs would no longer be sold by the underworld, and the violence that goes hand in hand with the drug trade today would disappear.

Drug-related violence is getting worse, too. In the United States, drug dealers armed with automatic weapons gun down whole families in bloody "object lessons" to demonstrate their power. In 1989, when the government of Colombia tried to crack down on the production and export of cocaine, . the local drug lords actually declared war on the government! They backed up their statement with force, murdering judges and government officials and launching a series of terrorist attacks on the Colombian citizens.

Alcohol harms the body, yet it's legal, say the backers of drug legalization. Why shouldn't drugs be legal, too, and the choice be left up to the individual? Billions of dollars would be saved in law enforcement, and billions in revenues could be collected with taxes similar to those the government receives on all liquor and cigarette sales.

Yet making drugs legal would probably lead to an increase in the numbers of drug users and addicts. That has been the experience in Great Britain. Moreover, the tax revenues from the legalized drugs would give the government a motive to maintain the addict population—much like the current situation in the tobacco and alcohol industries. Perhaps legalization of drug use could be justified by channeling the tax revenues from the industry and some of the savings from the reduction of law enforcement costs into research on cures on drug and other addictions.

Would this be ethical? At present, most Americans would say no. But the debate continues as the drug war drags on.

Further Reading

Barnes, Deborah M. "The Biological Tangle of Drug Addiction." *Science*, July 22, 1988, pp. 415–417.

Barun, Ken and Philip Bashe. *How To Keep the Children You Love Off Drugs.* New York: Atlantic Monthly Press, 1988.

Berger, Gilda. *Addiction: Its Causes, Problems, and Treatments.* New York: Franklin Watts, 1982.

Hodgkinson, Liz. *Addictions: What they are—Why they happen—How to Help.* Wellingborough, England: Thorsons Publishing Group, 1986.

Kagan, Daniel. "How America Lost Its First Drug War." *Insight,* November 20, 1989, pp. 8–17.

Nadelmann, Ethan A. "Drug Prohibition in the United States: Costs, Consequences, and Alternatives." *Science*, September 1, 1989, pp. 939–946.

Zuckerman, Mortimer B. "The Enemy Within." *U.S. News & World Report,* September 11, 1989, p. 91.

For More Information

DARE
(Drug Abuse Resistance Education)
Los Angeles Police Department
P.O. Box 30158
Los Angeles, CA 90030

The Just Say No Foundation
1777 North California Blvd.
Suite 200
Walnut Creek, CA 94596
(800) 258-2766

Project LEAD
(Leadership, Experience and
Development)
Quest International
6655 Sharon Woods Blvd.
Columbus, OH 43229
(800) 446-2800

Youth to Youth
700 Bryden Road
Columbus, OH 43215

REFERENCE

Illegal Drugs

"I remember," Julio says, taking quick, nervous puffs from his cigarette, "when I was a little kid, maybe eight or nine, and I used to take the garbage out for my mother, I'd always see tubes from airplane glue under the stairwell in our apartment house and in the alley out back. At first, glue just meant building models to me. But I'd see people sniffing it, under the stairwell. I was curious, and one day I tried it. It made me feel like I was in a trance. It wasn't really exciting, but I did it again and again. Until we moved, and in the new neighborhood people weren't into glue and I didn't see the empty tubes to remind me any more.

"I didn't intend to get into drugs, but my friends played a trick on me at a party. They gave me a cigarette and said it was just regular tobacco, rolled up in cigarette paper. It made me feel funny, like time was slowed down. I didn't really like the feeling, but when my friends told me it was a marijuana cigarette, I told them it was a cool feeling because I wanted to be part of the crowd. After that, when I'd hang out with my friends, we'd either smoke reefers or drink beer. Sometimes I'd get so sick my friends had to carry me home. But I kept doing it.

"When I was about fourteen, I started experimenting with all kinds of drugs. LSD—we called it 'acid'—I didn't like what it did to my mind, but I liked the energy it gave me. That and snorting cocaine. I could dance at the discos and meet girls on the dance floor and never get tired. But I wasn't hooked, you know. I could stop it any time I wanted."

Julio goes on about the jobs he lost, the pressures, and the white powder he learned to inject when he wanted to forget his troubles for a while. "My wife left me when I started doing heroin," he says. "But she came back when I went on the program, the methadone. I stayed clean for almost a year." "Clean" is a relative term; he mentions that while he was on the drug-treatment program, he stayed away from heroin but still smoked pot—"to tide me over the rough spots"—and started smoking crack "now and then." He grew irritable and suspicious, imagining that his wife was flirting with other men behind his back. She left him again after the last beating he gave her, and he dropped out of the drug-treatment program. Now he's buying heroin on the street again. "Too much stress," he mumbles . . .

Maureen would be indignant if anyone called her a drug addict, and she has never bought or used an illegal drug in her life. It's just that she finds it hard to get through the day without a few cups of coffee to wake her up, a couple of Valiums to calm her down when problems arise, and then some Seconal to help her get to sleep at night. Her family doctor first prescribed a tranquilizer and a sedative to help her get over the bad time after her parents were killed in a car crash. She liked the dreamy feeling they gave her, and she persuaded her doctor to write a few refills for her prescriptions because she still felt "nervous." Eventually he refused to continue, so Maureen just found another doctor. Over the years, new problems arose, each to be solved by some "magic pill." Now she has a prescription for Percodan for "back spasms" from one doctor, Seconal for insomnia from another. She found herself dozing off at the wheel of the car, so another doctor prescribed Ritalin for her "narcolepsy." Still another is treating her migraine headaches with Fiorinal. Maureen's daughter never brings friends home after school any more, explaining that "Mommy's not feeling well." She has learned that Mommy can't be depended on—sometimes she is sweet and loving, but she flies into a rage for no reason at all . . .

Drugs That Are Abused

More than one hundred illegal drugs are abused in our country today, according to the U.S. Drug Enforcement Administration. It has divided these and the legal drugs of abuse into five main groups:

1. *narcotics*—including codeine, heroin, methadone, morphine, opium
2. *depressants*—including barbiturates, methaqualone (Quaalude), and tranquilizers like Librium and Valium, as well as alcohol
3. *stimulants*—including amphetamines and cocaine, as well as nicotine and caffeine
4. *hallucinogens*—including LSD, mescaline, PCP
5. *cannabis*—including hashish, marijuana

Except for PCP, the hallucinogens are generally considered to be addictive. The addictive drugs basically fall into two main categories: stimulants ("uppers") and depressants ("downers"). Stimulants act on the central nervous system (the brain and spinal cord) to increase the rate of firing of nerve cells. The user has feelings of well-being, energy, and confidence. There is usually a price to pay, though, when the effects of the drug wear off and the "crash" follows. The name "depressants" may seem a little confusing. Who would want to take a drug to feel depressed? Actually the term doesn't pertain to the mood but rather to the effects on the central nervous system. Depressants act to inhibit neuron firing. Some of the nerve cells affected are involved in inhibitions and other checks on behavior. Under the influence of the drug, worries and tensions fade away, and the user feels good—relaxed, mellow, or even high. The drugs of groups one and two are depressants, and those of groups three and five are stimulants.

The table on pages 182–189 summarizes the various drugs that are commonly abused—what they are, how they work, and the effects they produce.

Narcotics

For most people, the ultimate drug abuser is the heroin addict who sticks needles of "dope," "junk," or "smack" into his arms. Ironically, when heroin was first introduced as a cough medicine in 1898, it was thought to be safe and nonaddictive. The new drug was the "heroine" that would save people from the dangers of addiction to morphine and opium. Eventually it was realized that heroin is just as addictive and twice as powerful as morphine. Laws were passed against it, but growing numbers of people continued buy and use it illegally.

The term *narcotic* comes from a Greek work meaning "to numb." The narcotics, made from the milky sap in the unripe seeds of the opium poppy plant, relieve pain, calm and numb the body and mind, and also create a dreamlike feeling of euphoria or happiness. Heroin and the other opiate drugs are chemically similar to the body's endorphins, and they attach to the endorphin receptors in the neurons in the brain. Their effect is more intense than that of the natural pain-killers, but tolerance to the drug builds up when narcotics are used frequently. The continual filling of the opiate receptors may cause some of the receptors to shut down, so that the drug cannot have as great an effect on nerve transmission. Or new receptors may be created, and these must also be filled in order to produce the same high. Gradually, the user must take more and more of the drug to get the same effect. Other chemical adjustments, as the body attempts to adapt to the constant supply of drugs, result in unpleasant withdrawal symptoms when the drug is stopped.

Infections, hepatitis, and AIDS are real concerns for addicts who share needles or use ones that are not properly sterilized. Sixty percent of intravenous drug abusers are thought to be infected with the AIDS virus.

Overdosing is another real problem for their heroin user because street heroin is a real gamble. Often other ingredients are added, like baby powder, milk powder, or other drugs (which may be dangerous), and the user never knows how pure the "fix" is. A mild overdose will cause the addict to fall asleep, but a heavy overdose can result in convulsions, coma, and death.

A synthetic narcotic, *methadone,* is a highly addictive opiatelike drug. But when it is given to a heroin addict in a dose too low to produce a high, it blocks the effects of heroin and helps to control the addict's craving for it. In a way, supervised methadone maintenance programs for heroin addicts substitute one addiction for another. But they permit addicts to lead a relatively normal life, without the need to turn to crime to support their drug habit.

Several other opiatelike drugs have been produced. Meperidine (Demerol) is a widely prescribed pain-killer that can be abused. The narcotics also include codeine, Percodan, and Darvon.

Barbiturates and Tranquilizers

Barbiturates and tranquilizers are called sedative-hypnotics. They calm the body (the sedative effect) and cause sleep (the hypnotic effect). Barbiturates do not come from the poppy plant, but are derived from the chemical barbituric acid. Since the first barbiturate (barbital) was formulated in the early 1900s, almost 2500 others have been developed. More than a dozen of these are still used today to treat conditions such as anxiety, epilepsy, high blood pressure, insomnia, and peptic ulcers. (Barbiturate-induced sleep is quite different from normal sleep. Barbiturate users do not dream as much and sometimes have a groggy hangover-type headache when they wake up.) The most commonly abused barbiturates are amobarbital (Amytal), pentobarbital (Nembutal), and secobarbital (Seconal).

Barbiturates act as a depressant on the central nervous system, apparently by interacting with the neurotransmitter gamma-aminobutyric acid (GABA). GABA molecules attach to nerve cells and slow down the production of other neurotransmitters. This decrease in available neurotransmitters decreases the firings of the nerve cells, causing brain activity to slow down.

Tranquilizers are another chemical class of depressants, which were developed as safer alternatives to the barbiturates, to produce a calming, sedative effect. Two of the most common tranquilizers are Valium and Librium. It is estimated that 10 percent of all adults take one of these two drugs, and two-thirds of them are women.

Barbiturates and tranquilizers can be very useful in helping people cope with an immediate crisis, but only when used for a short time. Unfortunately, many who use them become hooked and continue using them for extended periods of time. One-third of all drug overdose deaths are barbiturate overdoses, many of which are unintentional—especially when barbiturates are mixed with alcohol, which magnifies the depressive effects.

Methaqualone, or Quaalude, is another popular depressant drug of abuse. This synthetic drug is not chemically similar to barbiturates but produces some of the same effects. Quaaludes were first marketed in the mid-sixties as a sleep medication and were thought not to be addictive. However, dependency can develop with regular use.

Cocaine

When the Spaniards arrived in South America in the sixteenth century, they found that the Indians chewed the leaves of the coca plant. (This isn't the same as the cocoa plant from which cocoa and chocolate are extracted.) A substance in the leaves seemed to fill the users with added energy and also curbed their appetite. The conquistadors quickly recognized the advantages of the drug and encouraged the Indians to grow and use the coca plant so that they would work harder on less food.

Cocaine is one of the most powerful stimulants. Although it was once considered nonaddictive, it is actually one of the most addictive of all drugs. In one laboratory experiment, for example, monkeys who were taught to press a lever to get an injection of cocaine chose to take the drug in preference to all other activities—including eating, drinking, sleeping, and mating. They gave themselves doses continuously until they went into convulsions and died. (In other experiments, monkeys dosed themselves with nicotine or with amphetamines just as single-mindedly; but monkeys trained to take heroin were not as obsessed with the drug. They worked for heroin doses, but they stopped to eat and sleep. With alcohol, the addiction was even weaker.)

Experiments like these could not be conducted on humans, but researchers have gained some idea of the relative addictive powers of drugs through studies of addicts. It seems that in real life the situation is far more complex. One study indicated that nine out of ten people who tried cigarettes went on to become addicted; but only one in six who tried crack (a purified form of cocaine that can be smoked or injected) became addicted. For alcohol, the addiction rate was only one in ten. When addicts were asked how hard it was to stop using various drugs, most of them said heroin was the most difficult to stop, with cigarettes a very close second. Next came alcohol, and finally, cocaine.

Cocaine stimulates the central nervous system, filling the user with energy, as well as suppressing hunger. It causes the heart to beat faster, blood vessels to constrict, and blood pressure to rise; adrenaline builds up, and the user experiences a feeling of urgency typical of a "fight or flight" reaction.

Until the 1970s, cocaine users in the United States generally inhaled or "snorted" the drug through their noses. Taken in this way, it passes through the delicate mucous lining of the nose into the bloodstream and in three minutes reaches the brain, bringing a feeling of alertness, sharpness, and happiness. Cocaine in a more purified form called freebase can also be injected or smoked, producing an almost immediate "rush" of euphoria. (It takes cocaine thirty seconds to reach the brain when injected and fifteen seconds when smoked.) Do-it-yourself freebasing (heating cocaine with a flammable substance like ether to separate the drug from salts and other materials) can be a dangerous activity, as comedian Richard Pryor found out when he was badly burned after trying this.

The fire hazard was eliminated when huge amounts of crack hit the streets. Crack is a type of freebase cocaine that comes "ready to use," without any need to handle flammable substances. It gets its name from the crackling sound it makes when it is heated (usually in a glass pipe or sprinkled on a marijuana cigarette). The high the crack user experiences is more immediate—it gets to the brain in eight to ten seconds—and intense than the rush from snorting cocaine, but it lasts for only a few minutes.

As heroin addicts learned about the hazards of AIDS, many of them switched to crack. Ironically, some of them inject this drug, too, and their danger is even greater. Because the high from an injection of crack is so much briefer than that from heroin (a few minutes versus a few hours), intravenous crack users typically draw some blood back and reinject the drug, again and again—multiplying the chances for an exchange of infected blood if the needles are shared. Crack users are also more likely to engage in impulsive, unprotected sexual activity, which can spread the AIDS virus. Still another danger is presented by the tendency of growing numbers of cocaine users to inject heroin to ease the pain of the brutal low that sets in when the cocaine high wears off.

Cocaine works through the body's pleasure system by causing the production of an increased amount of the neurotransmitters dopamine and norepinephrine. Dopamine stimulates signals concerning eating and sex, and it helps produce feelings of energy and invigoration. Norepinephrine tones up various body systems to prepare for emergencies. These neurochemicals signal an urgency in the body that makes cocaine use seem like the most important thing in the user's life.

Cocaine not only causes a stimulation of neurons in the brain but also, as we have seen, prevents the brain from calming down again by blocking the normal reabsorption of neurotransmitters such as dopamine, norepinephrine, and serotonin. At first, there are feelings of excitement and euphoria as nerve cells are overstimulated. But gradually the neurotransmitters break down before there has been enough time to produce a new supply. Then comes the "crash," and the user feels irritable and depressed. Taking more cocaine depletes the neurotransmitters even more.

Chronic cocaine users often have severe mood swings. They are unable to concentrate, and they suffer from insomnia, loss of appetite, nervous twitches, severe headaches, bleeding noses (continued snorting causes damage to the mucous membranes in the nose), cold sweats, and paranoia—they constantly think everyone is out to get them. Cocaine use can also lead to sudden and unprovoked outbreaks of violent behavior.

Cocaine withdrawal appears to take place in three distinct stages. In the first stage the addict crashes. Depression, fatigue, and an intense craving begin. By the end of the first stage, the addict feels exhausted, but unable to sleep. Some turn to other drugs like alcohol or tranquilizers or narcotics to help unwind, which can lead to dependencies on other drugs as well.

The second stage lasts for several weeks. Craving gradually decreases. Sleep patterns become more normal. Depression decreases. However, at about the middle of this stage, the person becomes *anhedomic*—unable to experience normal pleasures in life and feeling bored all the time. Anhedonia is a major cause of relapse.

If the person progresses to the third stage of withdrawal, he or she becomes more and more able to experience pleasure and does not suffer from depression or low moods as much. However, the craving for the drug can still come and go.

The recent concern about drugs in America has been highlighted by cocaine abuse by sport figures and other celebrities. Drug abuse among athletes is nothing new, but in the past, when the drug of choice was alcohol or amphetamines, the problem usually went undetected. The athletes' personal lives may have slowly deteriorated, but the change in their bodies was so gradual that it did not affect their performance very much. With cocaine, however, the effects of the addiction often become noticeable within a single season. Even more shocking is the fact that a cocaine overdose can kill— suddenly, by a stroke or a heart attack. The danger is unpredictable: the strength of cocaine, like other street drugs, can vary greatly, and, in addition, a person's susceptibility to the effects of the drug can change. So any dose—even the first one a person ever takes or an amount that seems to be just a user's regular dose—may turn out to be a fatal overdose. Sudden death from cocaine use has already cut off the careers of several popular athletes, and each occurrence made nationwide headlines.

Amphetamines

Amphetamines ("uppers," "pep pills," or "speed") were popular drugs of abuse in the 1960s. The first amphetamines were created by chemists in the late 1800s. Originally used to treat narcolepsy, a sleeping disorder, amphetamines were also prescribed for energy, for helping people to stay awake, and for weight reduction. During World War II, amphetamines played an important role in keeping the soldiers alert and ready for action. By the 1970s, there were more than thirty different kinds. But as doctors became aware of the negative effects of the drugs and their addictive potential, tight legal restrictions were placed on their use.

Like cocaine, amphetamines are believed to work by upsetting the balance of the brain chemical dopamine. At first, the drug produces a high, and it also causes the heart rate and breathing rate to speed up and the blood pressure to rise. But within a couple of hours, the high wears off and a depressing low follows as the continued stimulation depletes the brain's dopamine reserves. The user is prompted to take another "upper" to avoid the low. By bedtime, he or she may be too revved up to sleep. It is common for amphetamine addicts to be addicted to barbiturates as well. In a vicious circle, they take "uppers" to perk them up in the morning and "downers" to unwind and go to sleep at night. The constant roller-coaster ups and downs of these drugs can be hard on the body. Physical health deteriorates, and behavior and personality change. Long-term use of amphetamines can result in aggressiveness, impaired judgment, mood swings, panic attacks, paranoia, and hallucinations.

In the 1960s, speed (methamphetamine, or Methedrine) was a popular amphetamine among drug abusers. "Speed freaks" often injected themselves several times a day in a drug spree called a run. The run could last up to a week with no sleep. Then the speed addicts would crash and sleep for a day or two before beginning another run. Because of the severity of its effects and the total absorption speed produces, some experts consider it one of the most dangerous drugs.

With the tightening of controls on amphetamines, speed fell out of fashion. But drug experts fear that it is now in the process of a spectacular comeback. In a new crystal form called ice, which can be smoked like crack, methamphetamine has spread from Japan and South Korea to Hawaii and is now gaining a foothold on the mainland United States. Like crack, ice rapidly gets to the brain and produces an almost immediate high, but the high lasts much longer—from seven to thirty hours, compared to only twenty to thirty minutes for crack. A $50 "paper" of ice (a cellophane packet containing a tenth of a gram), good for one or two hits, is thus more economical than crack in the long run. The high it produces is a jittery, "wired" feeling, and the user has the impression of being much more energetic and efficient. (The drug has become very popular among workaholics in Asia, whose jobs involve long hours and high stress.) The high from ice is followed by a crash said to be even worse than the low crack users experience.

Drug users often become violent. (In Honolulu, police report that ice is involved in about 70 percent of spouse-abuse cases.) Dependence on methamphetamine develops quickly, and the periods between drug use are plagued by craving for it. Ice can cause irregular heartbeat and respiration, convulsions, weight loss, and insomnia; prolonged use can produce psychological disorders and fatal damage to the lungs and kidneys.

Ironically, success in the current drug war, which is focused mainly on cocaine, may result in a more rapid spread of ice. Unlike cocaine, which is produced in a complicated process from naturally grown raw materials available only in certain parts of the world, methamphetamine can be produced in a lab from readily available chemicals—anywhere. How far this new drug menace will spread is not yet known. Representative Charles Rangel, chairman of the House Select Committee on Narcotics Abuse and Control, remarked at a hearing late in 1989, "This is our chance to get ahead of the curve and not make the same mistake that we made in dealing with the rise of crack several years ago."

Marijuana

Up to a few years ago, many authorities considered marijuana relatively harmless. But gradually, studies have revealed disturbing effects. A study released inn 1987, for example, examined the long-term effects of "pot" smoking. In 1974, groups of marijuana smokers and nonsmokers were tested for physical and psychological differences. At that time, both groups displayed similar test results. However, when the subjects were retested in 1986, habitual pot users were found to have more problems concentrating, remembering information, and learning new things. More often the pot smokers had taken manual labor jobs as opposed to jobs that required a lot of mental activity. Heavy pot smokers were also less outgoing and tended to be isolated and alienated. The American Medical Association declared: "There is no doubt at all that marijuana is a dangerous drug, with great potential for serious harm to young Americans."

Marijuana users smoke the leaves, stem, or flowering tops of a wild weed, the *Cannabis sativa* hemp plant, in a loosely rolled cigarette called a joint or a reefer, or in a pipe; sometimes it is eaten, mixed in foods like brownies. Marijuana leaves contain over 400 chemicals that are turned into almost 2,000 different products when they are burned. THC or delta-9-tetrahydrocannabinol is the chemical that produces the marijuana high, which can last from two to four hours. The marijuana used in the United States today has much more THC than it used to: about 50 milligrams (5 percent) in an average joint, compared to 2 milligrams (0.2 percent) back in the 1960s. Some types can have as much as 14 percent!

THC remains in the liver, brain, and other parts of the body for as much as a month. In addition to a dreamy, relaxing high, it produces a number of negative effects including a decrease in reaction time and physical coordination (driving skill is impaired by pot smoking just as it is by alcohol intoxication), dry mouth and throat, and anxiety attacks. Habitual marijuana users are often called burnouts or space cadets because the drug slows down mental faculties and produces lethargy and a shortened attention span. Medical studies have found that smoking marijuana can increase chances of lung cancer even more than cigarettes. One marijuana joint is equivalent in tar and other carcinogens to more than a pack of cigarettes. Marijuana also lowers the body's immunity by decreasing the number of disease-fighting white blood cells. Evidence suggests as well that boys who smoke marijuana regularly before puberty may not have normal sexual development.

Long-term marijuana smoking may cause a reduction in the levels of natural opiates in the body, as well as decreased amounts of the neurotransmitter norepinephrine. An addictive cycle can develop where the brain craves additional doses of marijuana to resupply the depleted brain chemicals.

Treatment of Drug Addiction

If drug use is occasional, treatment can consist of bringing the drug user to peer counseling support groups, such as Cocaine Anonymous, Narcotics Anonymous, and Drugs Anonymous. These groups are made up of ex-addicts who share their stories and help each other fight their drug addictions and remain drug free. Educational and nutritional information are an integral part of the programs. At first rehabilitating addicts may need to attend meetings every day; then they may taper off to once a week or less.

When a drug problem is more serious, a professional outpatient program that lasts from four to six months might be preferred. Nearly eight out of ten who seek treatment enter outpatient programs. During the day, the drug user goes to school or work and then goes to the clinic afterward. At the clinic he or she receives individual and group therapy, as well as educational support. After about six months, the patient is reevaluated. If recovery seems established, an aftercare program of six months to a year with weekly counseling follows.

If these methods fail, or if drug use is very serious, an inpatient program might be necessary. The drug user is taken completely out of the old environment and placed in a new setting, sometimes in a hospital, sometimes in a residential facility. Often it is set in a countrylike environment with acres of trees and outdoor activities. The Hazelden rehabilitation program, for example, is set on 288 acres in Minnesota. These programs typically last for a month.

Detoxification is necessary with all heavily addicted drug users. The addict can go cold turkey or can be gradually weaned off the drugs. Most prefer the gradual weaning because going cold turkey can be quite severe, especially if from cocaine, heroin, or amphetamines. Constant medical supervision is necessary.

After the patient is drug free, extensive therapy, both group and individual, follows, along with educational classes dealing with the hazards of drugs. The importance of nutrition and physical activity is also stressed. After the month-long inpatient program is over, the patient returns home but should continue in an outpatient aftercare program or with a support group for up to a year.

If an inpatient program is not enough, the drug user may need to seek long-term treatment in a therapeutic community (TC), which can last from a year to two and a half years. The first TC, Synanon, was started by Charles Dederich in 1958 in Santa Monica, California. TC programs are extremely regimented and strict; they strive to break down the addict's ego and force him or her to seek help and depend on others. Once they admit they need help, addicts are constantly encouraged as long as they display the "correct" behavior. Supporters of programs like this believe that only a "spiritual transformation" will enable a person to remain drug free.

All treatment programs utilize one or more of three basic approaches to drug rehabilitation. The inpatient and outpatient programs usually implement a detoxification approach, which is to get the addict off the drug he or she is addicted to. This approach is most effective when accompanied by the second approach of extensive psychological counseling. Therapeutic communities help restructure an addict's life by removing him or her from a drug environment and making it possible, through peer support, to relearn new drug-free behavior.

The third main approach is the maintenance approach, which is used especially in narcotics addictions. It goes on the assumption that it is very hard for an addict to remain drug free. A more practical goal is to replace the harmful drug with a less harmful substance. In this way the addict will not be part of the drug-crime cycle. In heroin treatment, for example, methadone is administered at a clinic on a daily basis. Of course, all maintenance programs require extensive psychological counseling as well.

To some people, this approach may seem a bit crazy—substituting one addiction for another. (Methadone is addictive!) But methadone has many advantages over heroin. Methadone is taken orally in a liquid form, not injected like heroin. This difference is especially important in view of the AIDS crisis since one way the disease is spread is by IV drug users sharing contaminated needles. Another advantage is that a methadone high does not disrupt a person's normal life, and it lasts for twenty-four hours without any withdrawal symptoms between doses. In addition, methadone maintenance costs society only a few thousand dollars per patient each year, compared to the cost of the crimes an addict may commit to come up with the $40,000 or more needed each year to keep up a heroin habit. Imprisoning an addict, too, can cost ten to twenty times as much as methadone maintenance. Research indicates that methadone does cut down on crimes, and the patient can function well at a job and interact with others.

Methadone works by filling up the opiate receptors in the brain, creating a sense of well-being, although it does not produce the dreamlike high of other opiates. But methadone maintenance can be a lifetime affair, and there are various side effects as well. Researchers are trying to find better drugs that can be used to help addicts break free of drug dependency. LAAM (levo-alpha-acetylmethadol), for example, works for several days.

But researchers are developing new drugs that will not substitute one addiction for another. Several drugs already look promising for breaking narcotics addiction. One is clonidine, a high-blood-pressure drug. It helps to restore the depleted levels of norepinephrine in the brains of addicts and reduces their craving for the narcotic. Clonidine is not addictive and does not create a high of its own, but it can produce negative side effects such as low blood pressure and sleeping disorders. Another experimental drug, naltrexone, blocks the euphoric high of heroin by preventing the heroin

66

molecules from attaching to the opiate receptors. Naltrexone is not addictive, and it does not produce a high.

Antidepressants such as desipramine (Norpramin, Pertofrane), imipramine (Tofranil), trazodone, and lithium have shown some promise in treating cocaine abusers. In one experimental study, for example, 60 percent of the subjects given desipramine were able to abstain from cocaine for at least three weeks. Antidepressants work somewhat similarly to cocaine but are not addictive and help to restore the depleted supplies of dopamine. They also reduce the cocaine-induced oversensitivity of nerve cells to neurotransmitters, so that a cocaine user who takes the drug while being treated with antidepressants does not feel the usual high. Combining antidepressants with tryptophan and tyrosine, amino acids that the body can use to make the neurotransmitters serotonin, dopamine, and norepinephrine, seems even more effective. Anti-epilepsy drugs such as carbamazepine help the recovering cocaine addict by blocking the erratic nerve-cell firing that cocaine use produces. Bromocriptine, a drug used in the treatment of Parkinson's disease, tricks the body by acting like dopamine to stimulate the dopamine receptors. In experimental tests, this drug worked more quickly than antidepressants to help reduce cocaine craving. Other drugs that have been tested are sertalene, which blocks the re-uptake of serotonin by nerve cells in the brain; buspirone, an antianxiety drug; chlorpromazine, an antipsychotic drug; and mazindol, an anti-obesity drug.

Buprenorphine, a pain-killing drug, suppresses the cravings for both heroin and cocaine and also blocks the high from heroin. Its molecule has two parts: one that stimulates the same opiate receptors to which heroin binds and another part that blocks these opiate receptors. In low doses buprenorphine produces a pleasant feeling (though not a euphoric high), but in higher doses its blocking effect becomes stronger. It is especially promising for people addicted to both heroin and cocaine. Unlike methadone, buprenorphine cannot become a substitute addiction, and it is also safer because its blocking effect prevents lethal overdoses. A lozenge form that dissolves in the mouth is now being developed for easier use.

Whatever treatment approach is used, aftercare programs can make all the difference when it comes to backsliding. The Veterans Hospital in Seattle found that only 30 percent of the patients who completed the nine-month aftercare program returned to their old drug-using lives. Of those who did not complete the aftercare program, 80 percent went back to drugs.

Aftercare programs generally include meetings once a week to discuss ways to continue drug free. Recovering addicts learn to identify environmental triggers that can cause them to backslide— like old friends who do drugs or places and things that are associated with drugs— and learn how to deal with and overcome them. Most aftercare programs encourage the patient to join an AA-type support group. Patients are urged to go to a meeting every day for the first three months, and then to continue regularly for the rest of their lives. These self-help support groups make the most sense in aftercare treatment because they are free and offer peer support and encouragement.

Further Reading

"Alcohol and Drug Abuse." *World Book Health & Medicine,* 1989, pp. 235–238.

Barnes, Deborah M. "Breaking the Cycle of Addiction." *Science,*August 26, 1988, pp. 1029–1030.

Barun, Ken and Philip Bashe. *How To Keep the Children You Love Off Drugs.* New York: Atlantic Monthly Press, 1988.

Berger, Gilda. *Addiction: Its Causes. Problems, and Treatments.* New York: Franklin Watts, 1982.

"Effects of Commonly Abused Drugs." *World Almanac,* 1989, pp. 213–215.

Grinspoon, Lester and James B. Bakalar. *Cocaine: A Drug and Its Social Evolution.* New York: Basic Books, 1985.

Hodgkinson, Liz. *Addictions: What they are—Why they happen—How to Help.* Wellingborough, England: Thorsons Publishing Group, 1986.

Straus, Hal. "From Crack To Ecstasy." *American Health,* June 1987, pp. 50–54.

Washton, Arnold M. and Donna Boundy. *Crack: What You Need To Know.* Hillside, N.J.: Enslow Publishers, 1989.

Wilbur, Robert. "Drugs that Fight Coke," *American Health,* June 1987, pp. 44–49.

Helpful Organizations

Cocaine Hotline:
1-800-COCAINE

The American Council for Drug Education
204 Monroe St.
Rockville, MD 20850
(301) 294-0600

Cocaine Anonymous
World Service Office
P.O. Box 1367
Culver City, CA 90239
(213) 559-5800

Cocanon Family Groups
East Coast Office:
P.O. Box 1080, Cooper Station
New York, NY 10276-1080
(212) 713-5133
West Coast Office:
(213) 859-2206

Drug Referral Hotline
(800) 662-HELP

Hazelden Education Materials
Box 176
Center City, MN 55012
(800) 328-9000

Narcotics Anonymous World Service Office
P.O. Box 9999
Van Nuys, CA 91409
(818) 780-3951

Narcotics Education, Inc.
6830 Laurel St.
Washington, DC 20012-9979

National Clearinghouse on Drug Abuse Information
P.O.Box 416
Kensington, MD 20795
(301) 443-6500

National Institute on Drug Abuse
Prevention Branch, 5600
Fishers Lane, Room 10A-30
Rockville, MD 20857

Alcohol

Alcohol has been around for a long time. Archaeologists have uncovered ancient Mesopotamian scenes from 4200 B.C. showing alcoholic drinks being made. There is other evidence that beer and wine may have been drunk up to 8,000 years ago. Today alcoholic beverages are still a normal part of life for many people. In America, more than three-quarters of all adult men and three-fifths of adult women drink alcohol, at least occasionally. Americans consume over 400 million gallons of liquors, 570 million gallons of wine, and nearly six billion gallons of beer each year!

But alcohol is more than a beverage; it is one of the oldest drugs known. Although alcoholic beverages probably were first drunk because they were safer than water from local waterholes, they have also been used in religious ceremonies and for medicinal purposes. Alcohol abuse probably goes back as far into human history as its use as a beverage. It can change the state of the user's mind and has sedating and pain-reducing effects on the body.

Drinking in moderation is a socially accepted way of helping people to relax and enjoy themselves at parties, or forget about work and life's troubles for a while. Most people enjoy the mildly pleasant effects of moderate drinking and know when to stop drinking. They realize that drinking too much will get them drunk and that they may act foolishly while intoxicated, may become sick and vomit, and are likely to suffer from hangovers the next

71

day. They realize, too, that long-term heavy drinking can interfere with their normal lives and lead to serious health problems.

But some people drink to become intoxicated. They drink a lot at a time, and they drink often. After a while, they may find themselves craving a drink all the time or may be unable to stop drinking once they start. This excessive drinking can begin to cause problems in their lives. Heavy drinkers may miss work or school because they are constantly hung over. They may get in trouble with the law or do poorly at work or school because alcohol affects their physical and mental abilities and their behavior. When alcohol seems to control a person's life in this way, he or she is called an *alcoholic*.

Most people picture an alcoholic as a bum lying in a gutter. But less than 3 percent of alcoholics are skid-row types; most are leading ordinary lives—at least, most of the time.

Profile of an Alcoholic

Alcoholics often drink for years without developing any problems. They may have a drink or two to relax like other social drinkers. At first, the person likes the feelings that drinking brings and can control the times and amount of drinking. Gradually, however, this control is lost. More and more the person begins to need and depend on alcohol to escape problems. This psychological dependence progresses to a physical dependence as well, and the alcoholic feels he or she cannot live without drinking.

Alcoholics become unable to control their desire to drink, and it becomes the center of their lives. An alcoholic can be hooked on any alcoholic beverage: hard liquor, beer, or wine. Even the frequency of drinking does not necessarily give an alcoholic away. Some can go for weeks at a time without drinking, whereas others drink to the point of passing out every day. The one thing they all have in common is that drinking disrupts their lives.

Not everyone who drinks will become an alcoholic. And not everyone who drinks heavily is necessarily an alcoholic, either. Experts estimate that there are about ten million alcoholics in America and another eight million problem drinkers, or people who drink too much. These problem drinkers may eventually moderate their drinking habits, or they may actually be alcoholics in very early stages. Two-thirds of all alcoholics are men.

What Is Alcoholism?

Society's views about why people drink too much have gone through many changes. The ancient Roman philosopher Seneca called continual drunkenness a form of insanity. Philadelphia doctor Benjamin Rush, one of the signers of the Declaration of Independence, concluded that continual drunkenness was a disease and that users were unable to control its habitual use. The only cure was total abstinence. In 1849 Magnus Huss, a Swedish physician, used the term alcoholism for the first time. The medical view of alcoholism as a kind of disease, however, was not shared by the general public, who considered it a character defect—a sin, not a sickness, which should be punished rather than treated. In the late 1940s, research by Dr. E. M. Jellinek of Yale University helped to sway public opinion to the medical view, which was endorsed by the American Psychiatric Association, the World Health Organization, and the American Medical Association. The 1982 opening of the Betty Ford Center and the frank admissions by admired celebrities like Betty Ford, Elizabeth Taylor, Liza Minelli, and Jason Robards that they were struggling with alcohol problems helped to change the public's attitude. In a 1987 Gallup poll, 87 percent of the people questioned believed alcoholism was a disease.

According to the American Medical Association, "Alcoholism is an illness characterized by preoccupation with alcohol and loss of control over its consumption such as to lead to intoxification if drinking is begun, by chronicity, by progression, and by tendency toward relapse." This definition indicates that alcoholism is a chronic disease that gets worse the more the

73

alcoholic drinks, and when the alcoholic tries to stop drinking, there is a very high likelihood that he or she will begin drinking again.

In 1987 the American Psychiatric Association agreed on three basic elements necessary to diagnose a drinker as an alcoholic:

1. *psychological element:* the person has an obsessive desire to drink
2. *physiological element:* the person has physical symptoms like hand tremors and blackouts
3. *behavioral element:* the person's drinking disrupts his or her personal and/or work life.

Alcohol and How It Works

All alcoholic drinks contain ethyl alcohol (ethanol). Ethanol is produced by a natural process called fermentation, which turns the sugar found in various foods like grapes, potatoes, corn, wheat, barley, sugarcane, and molasses into ethanol. The fermentation process continues until it is stopped or until a certain level of ethanol is reached. Fourteen percent ethanol is the highest concentration that fermentation can produce in an alcoholic beverage. When the beverage is heated, the alcohol evaporates and can be collected by a process called distillation. In this way, it is possible to obtain beverages with over 90 percent alcohol.

A glass of wine, a can of beer, and a mixed drink all have about the same amount of ethyl alcohol: half an ounce. When a person drinks an alcoholic beverage, the ethanol—a rather small molecule—is absorbed through the walls of the stomach and intestines into the bloodstream, which carries it to every part of the body including the brain. How quickly the alcohol is absorbed into the blood depends on many factors, such as how much food is in the stomach. (Food slows down the absorption of ethanol.)

How soon one feels alcohol's effects depends on the speed with which it is absorbed into the blood and also on the person's weight—the heavier the person, the longer it takes for the effects to be felt. A stomach enzyme, alcohol dehydrogenase, breaks down part of the alcohol before it is absorbed through the stomach wall. Recently researchers have discovered that women normally make less of this enzyme than men, and alcoholics make the least of all. If a nonalcoholic woman and a nonalcoholic man who have the same weight each drink the same amount of an alcoholic beverage, the woman will absorb one-third more alcohol, and her blood alcohol level will rise more rapidly. A similar drink will also hit an alcoholic faster and harder, and repeated alcohol abuse will be more likely to cause liver disease in a person with lower levels of the protective enzyme.

The body gets rid of a tenth of the absorbed alcohol through the breath, sweat, and urine. The rest is broken down, or metabolized, by the liver, which filters out chemicals that can be harmful to the body. The liver can break down about half an ounce of ethanol (or one drink) per hour. If more than one drink is consumed per hour, the ethanol concentration in the blood increases, and a backlog builds up for the liver to take care of.

In the brain, alcohol acts as a depressant, slowing down the activity of the neurons. The more alcohol in the blood, the greater the effect on the brain. One or two drinks can produce a calming, relaxing feeling. But after several drinks in a row, judgment is impaired, reactions slow down, and muscle coordination becomes impaired. Two and a half ounces of ethanol (five beers) drunk in an hour by a person of average weight will produce about a 10 percent alcohol concentration in the blood, which is the legal level of intoxication. Driving a car with this amount of alcohol in the blood could result in a drunk driving arrest, should the drinker be stopped by the police. Taking twelve drinks in an hour can turn off the breathing center in the brain, and person could go into a coma and die.

Surprisingly, some studies suggest that circumstances can influence how a person feels after drinking and can even affect the changes alcohol produces in the body. In an experiment where subjects were told they were taking part

75

in a beverage taste test, for example, those who *thought* they were drinking a vodka and tonic acted more aggressively and showed other typical effects of drunkenness than those who were told they were drinking plain tonic— even though some of the subjects who thought they had an alcoholic drink were given plain tonic and some of those who thought they were drinking only tonic actually had drinks spiked with vodka. In another study, a group of men who thought they were drinking alcohol showed a tendency for reduced heart rate, whether or not their belief was true. It seems that some of the physiological effects, at least of moderate drinking, are at least partly psychological effects, influenced by the surroundings and the person's expectations.

Most medical studies have concluded that moderate drinking is not harmful to humans. There is even some controversial evidence that an alcoholic drink a day might have some beneficial health effects. But the problems resulting from heavy drinking are undisputed. Ethanol in high concentrations disrupts the normal functioning of cells, impairing the flow of biochemicals and nutrients. Unlike other drugs, which act on specific receptors, ethanol can penetrate readily through cell membranes and affects all cells.

Researchers are trying to discover why ethanol has a sedating effect on the body. Steven Paul, at the national Institute of Mental Health, believes that a receptor site called the *GABA-benzodiazepine receptor* is involved. The neurotransmitter gamma-aminobutyric acid (GABA) has an inhibiting effect on neurons. When enough GABA molecules attach to the receptors of enough neurons, a sedating effect is produced and anxiety is reduced. The tranquilizers Valium and Librium belong to a chemical group called *benzodiazepines*. They produce a calming effect by attaching to the GABA receptors. Paul believes ethanol also acts on these GABA receptors and has demonstrated on rats that a drug that blocks activation of the GABA receptors also blocks the sedating effects of alcohol. (If researchers can develop a less toxic version of the drug he used, it could serve as a sobering up pill.)

Excessive drinking over a period of time produces tolerance—the alcohol drinker must take more to get the same effect. Withdrawal symptoms may occur once the alcoholic stops drinking, or between binges. Many alcoholics experience withdrawal symptoms even when they drink just a little less than usual. The most common withdrawal symptom is the hangover headache. Without alcohol in the system, the central nervous system goes into a rebound effect, and the alcoholic may experience nausea, cramps, tremors, and shakes.

Heavy drinking over a long period of time can produce much more serious effects, as well. In some alcohol addicts, withdrawal leads to *delirium tremens,* or DT's, characterized by hallucinations, mental confusion, seizures, trembling, and sometimes death. Serious alcohol withdrawal can actually be more difficult and dangerous than heroin withdrawal.

It doesn't take a very long for excessive drinking to begin to damage the body. After a few weeks of heavy drinking, the liver becomes less efficient, and damaging poisons build up. Heavy drinking affects nearly every system of the body; it can damage the major organs and impair their functions, can cause blood disorders such as anemia and high blood pressure, and has been liked to various forms of cancer. Even moderate alcohol use also greatly increases the risks of birth defects and mental retardation in children born to mothers who drank while pregnant.

The effects of alcohol on perception, reaction time, and coordination contribute to accidents on the road, on the water, and at work. Alcohol is involved in one-third to one-half of all murders, suicides, and accidental deaths. In fact, all told, alcohol kills more than 100,000 Americans every year. That's more than twenty-five times as many deaths as those caused by all illegal drugs combined! It is estimated that alcohol costs America 117 billion dollars a year from premature deaths, reduced output, and treatment of alcohol-related illnesses. In many countries in the world, alcohol abuse is one of the top health problems.

What Causes Alcoholism?

Why are some people able to drink alcohol occasionally and never develop an addiction to it while others cannot stop drinking? A long time ago, doctors noticed that alcoholism seems to run in families; over a hundred different studies have confirmed this finding. Until the 1970s it was generally thought that people started drinking because they learned this behavior at home—their parents drank, and very often they were neglected or abused by an alcoholic parent. More recent studies, though, suggest that alcoholism—or a tendency to develop it—might be inherited.

Several extensive studies of adopted children have revealed that biological sons of alcoholics are far more likely to become alcoholics themselves, regardless of whether their adoptive parents have drinking problems or not. In a Swedish study, for example, one-third of the biological sons of alcoholics became addicted to alcohol, compared to only one-tenth of the general public.

Studies at the University of California at San Diego revealed some apparently hereditary differences in the reaction to alcohol. Student volunteers were given unmarked drinks that looked, smelled, and tasted identical, but some contained alcohol and others did not. The students who had alcoholic fathers generally felt less drunk that those with nonalcoholic fathers. Even when blood alcohol levels were the same, the sons of alcoholics did better on eye-hand coordination tests than the sons of nonalcoholics. Various hormones that normally rise with alcohol intake (prolactin, cortisol, and adrenocorticotropic hormone) rose significantly less in the sons of alcoholics that in the sons of nonalcoholics. Forty percent of the sons of alcoholics showed this decrease in sensitivity to alcohol, versus only 10 percent of the sons of nonalcoholics. More recent tests have found similar results for the daughters of alcoholics.

Researchers believe that this decrease in sensitivity allows an individual to tolerate alcohol better than the average person, which makes it hard to learn when to stop drinking. The normal feedback signals such as slurring of speech and a loss of coordination take longer to be felt, and the person tends to drink larger quantities and more often. The habit of heavy drinking may become established in high school and college, when drinking is encouraged by friends.

Other studies have revealed abnormalities in the brain waves of alcoholics. Henry Beleiter of the State University of New York Health Science Center in Brooklyn found that even ex-alcoholics who had abstained for several years showed these abnormal brain waves. When he tested the children of alcoholics, he found that 30 to 35 percent of the sons of alcoholics had abnormal brain waves as well, compared to only 1 percent of the sons of nonalcoholics. Among sons of alcoholics who used alcohol to release their inhibitions, 89 percent had the abnormal brain waves. These findings have been corroborated by several other studies. Researchers are now following the cases of children who show the various alcoholic-indicating signs to see if they do indeed develop alcoholic behavior. They hope that differences in brain waves and biochemistry may eventually provide the basis for tests to pinpoint which people can drink safely and which are particularly at risk of developing alcohol addiction.

The idea that heredity contributes to alcoholism does not necessarily mean that one inherits alcoholic genes like the genes for hair or eye color. It is rather a tendency or predisposition toward developing a more general mental or chemical disorder, and alcoholism is just one of any number of possible symptoms. Other forms of drug addiction or compulsive behavior might just as easily arise, but alcohol is the most readily available as the choice of poison. The fact that many people suffer dual addictions may lend some support to this idea. In one study, more than one-third of alcoholics polled were addicted to other drugs as well. John Slade of New Jersey

Medical School has found that 70 to 80 percent of all alcohol abusers are smokers as well, and 20 percent of all smokers have a drinking problem.

An estimated 30 percent of all alcoholics have no family history of alcoholism. Therefore, most scientists feel that both genetic and environmental factors (nature and nurture) contribute to alcoholism. Studies by C. Robert Cloninger at Washington University in St. Louis have revealed two distinct types of alcoholics.

The first type, which included about 25 percent of those studied, drank heavily before they were twenty-five and were mostly men. They had gotten into trouble in school, at their jobs, or with the police. Often they began drinking on their own, without encouragement by their friends. These alcoholics tended to be aggressive and sometimes violent and had a very low success rate for treatment. The sons of this type of alcoholic were nine times more likely than normal to be alcoholics. Dr. Cloninger believes this type of alcoholism is strongly hereditary and calls the group *male-limited alcoholics*.

The second type fits the description of 75 percent of the alcoholics studied. These were men and women who didn't start to drink chronically until after age twenty-five. They typically had few problems with the police or with work and school. The children of this type of alcoholic were only twice as likely to become alcoholics themselves, and the success rate after treatment was much higher. Cloninger calls this type of alcoholism *milieu limited,* reflecting his belief that alcoholics of this type are born with a genetic predisposition for alcoholism, but it is triggered by continued heavy drinking.

If a tendency for alcoholism is indeed inherited, what specific factors determine this predisposition? One theory is that alcoholic-prone people inherit an enzyme deficiency that makes them unable to complete the series of chemical reactions involved in converting alcohol to harmless products. Another hereditary link may involve the endorphins and their receptors in the brain. Kenneth Blum and his colleagues at the University of Texas at San Antonio believes that alcoholics suffer from reduced levels of these natural opiates and drink compulsively to produce a sense of well-being. Studies of laboratory animals and human drinkers have revealed that heavy alcohol consumption raises endorphin levels at first, but after continued use the endorphin levels drop dramatically. As the alcoholic-prone drinker continues to indulge, the lowered levels of the brain opiate create an even greater desire to drink.

Dr. Blum suggests that there are three types of alcoholics. The *Type I* alcoholic is a *born alcoholic*. This individual is born with a deficiency in the endorphin system and drinks alcohol to compensate for the lower level of endorphins.

Type II alcoholics, or *stress-induced alcoholics,* start out as social drinkers, but heavy drinking due to environmental stress alters the brain chemistry by reducing endorphin levels and leads to temporary alcoholic behavior.

Type III alcoholics, or *drug-induced alcoholics,* were born with normal endorphin levels but develop a permanent endorphin deficiency due to excessive overdrinking, which develops into dependency and addiction to · alcohol.

Researchers believe that in the future it may be possible to help alcoholics avoid the craving for alcohol through manipulation of their brain chemistry by increasing endorphin levels or by slowing down the rate at which these natural opiates are broken down.

Studies at Texas A&M University have revealed another factor that may contribute to alcoholism. The research team, headed by Jack Nation, found that cadmium and lead caused laboratory rats to have a desire for alcohol. Normally rats will not drink even small amounts of alcohol, but when lead or cadmium was added to their normal food, the rats chose to drink alcohol over water! The Texas A&M researchers belief that the rats chose alcohol because they learned by trial and error that this drug helped to relieve the unpleasant feeling they experienced.

81

When humans consume lead or cadmium, they experience anxiety. The researchers think that this same mechanism may be contributing to alcoholism in humans because cadmium pollution of foods and drinking water is becoming a growing problem. Traces of this metal can also be found in tobacco.

Not all experts believe that alcoholism is a physical illness. The 1988 Supreme Court decision denying two veterans extension of educational benefits because their alcoholism was willful misconduct was based in part on the writings of Herbert Fingarette, a philosophy professor at the University of California at Santa Barbara. In a recent book, *Heavy Drinking: The Myth of Alcoholism As a Disease,* he declares that alcoholism begins when people unwittingly handle a problem with a drink. Gradually they work themselves over a period of years into drinking as a way to handle life, a tragic and destructive kind of life. It's very difficult to change.Many specialists believe that alcoholism is a learned behavior, with psychological and emotional factors as the main motivators. During childhood and adolescence, patterns are learned and established that can affect us for the rest of our lives. Overindulgence, abuse, lack of love, or numerous other factors can cause a growing child to develop a vulnerable and dependent personality. Many alcoholics have this type of personality. They have difficulty coping with stressful situations and turn to alcohol as a way to cover up or deal with insecurities. For them, alcohol tends to reduce inhibitions and ease tensions; if its use is encouraged by peers, drinking becomes an accepted way of coping with life's problems. Unfortunately, this dependence becomes more and more ingrained as time passes.

The attitudes of the community toward alcohol have a major influence on patterns of individual alcohol use and abuse. These views vary greatly among the different cultures and affect the rates of alcoholism for the community. For some groups, drinking wine at meals is a normal part of life; for others, it is an important part of religious rituals. Some cultures consider alcohol evil and regard users as criminals. These attitudes affect how a particular culture defines alcoholic behavior. In some South American cultures, for example, it is considered perfectly normal for people to become drunk at fiestas and miss work for several days afterward, whereas this type of behavior would be viewed as problem drinking in other cultures.

Biological differences may account for some of the cultural differences in attitudes toward alcohol. Three-quarters of the Orientals tested in several different studies experienced flushing and nausea when they drank even a small amount of alcohol. Jews also typically have higher rates of adverse reactions to alcohol and have been shown in some studies to have lower-than-average rates of alcoholism. American Indians and the Irish, on the contrary, have often been stereotyped as having high percentages of alcoholics. Many experts, however, feel that these social differences are only myths and point to the growing number of alcoholics in all groups.

Teenage Drinking

"I was like a runaway train, speeding dangerously out of control," teenage movie star Drew Barrymore wrote in her autobiography, *Little Girl Lost*. Both her father and her grandfather had been alcoholics, and she had started early. At seven Drew was pouring Bailey's Irish Cream over her ice cream, and at nine she was drinking with fast-track friends at nightclub parties. By the time she was fourteen she had spent time in a private rehabilitation hospital undergoing treatment for alcoholism and drug addiction, had emerged proudly dry and sober—and then had slipped back into drinking just a few months later. The humiliation propelled her into a suicide attempt that was really a call for help. Now, after another stay at the treatment center, she is attending Alcoholics Anonymous meetings, going for family therapy with her mother, and taking one day at a time.

The problems of celebrities often seem larger than life, but Drew Barrymore's story helped to spotlight the fact that problem drinking does not affect only adults; large and growing numbers of teenagers also use and abuse alcohol. The 1987 National Adolescent Student Health Survey, for example, found that 77 percent of eighth graders and 89 percent of tenth graders had tried alcohol; nearly a third said they had five or more drinks in one sitting during the previous two weeks.

Every state except Wyoming has a drinking age of twenty-one, but alcohol consumption has not really slowed down among teenagers and preteens. One problem is that many parents are not upset by their children's drinking. They think it is better than getting involved in drugs. Yet alcohol *is* a drug, and researchers have found that the earlier a child uses a dependence-producing drug, the higher the chances are that he or she will use other drugs and the greater the chance of experiencing drug-related health problems. Many young drinkers are involved in other addictions. Cocaine users drink alcohol when they crash, and alcohol users sometimes use other drugs to relieve hangovers.

Research has found that a good indicator for predicting the drinking habits of adolescents is to examine their parents' attitudes toward alcohol. Heavy-drinking adolescents more often than not come from families where one or both parents are heavy drinkers, or where both parents never drink. In the first case they learn from their parents' example. In the second case, the adolescent may be using drinking as a form of rebellion.

Young people receive mixed messages about alcohol. It is a socially accepted drug, but most think of it as a beverage rather than a drug. Television and movies glorify drinking. Characters throw up and pass out, but they never get hurt, and they end up as heroes. By the time a person is of legal drinking age, he or she will have seen alcohol being consumed over 75,000 times on TV and in the movies. The young adult will also have seen well over 100,000 beer commercials. These commercials glamorize the use of alcohol, and over one billion dollars is spent on beer and wine commercials every year!

Peer pressure is another huge factor in adolescent drinking. According to *Weekly Reader*, more than one-third of the fourth graders polled in a survey felt pressured by their friends to try alcohol, and more than one-fourth believed that classmates had tried drinking. By the time a student becomes a senior in high school, the peer pressure is even more apparent. Ninety-three percent of all high school seniors have tried alcohol, and more than two-thirds have consumed alcohol within the last month. Five percent drink every day, and 30 percent get drunk at least once a week. All together, five million adolescents (30 percent) have a drinking problem.

For many, college is the first time away from home, and college students typically experiment with types of behavior that may not have been approved of by their parents. In many colleges, alcohol is readily available, even though most of the students have not yet reached the legal drinking age. Perhaps one of the worst sides of college drinking is binge drinking, in which large quantities of alcohol are consumed at one time. Over two hundred young people die each year from alcohol overdose due to college and military drinking games. (A number of colleges have recently placed restrictions on the activities of fraternities and clubs after deaths related to excessive drinking.) Most college experimenters remain only occasional drinkers, but some continue to drink heavily long after college.

How to Tell if Someone Is an Alcoholic

During the early stages of alcoholism, it may be very difficult to find clear signs that an individual is an alcoholic rather than just an occasional drinker. Even family doctors may be unaware of their patient's alcoholism because alcoholics almost never admit they have a problem. They believe they can stop drinking whenever they want to.

There are many warning signs that alcohol may be beginning to control a person's life. These include sudden changes in attitude. Mild-tempered adolescents might begin to treat their parents with anger and contempt. Adults

85

may show distinct mood shifts. A happy-go-lucky, sober individual can become bad-tempered and vicious while drinking. A sudden decrease in performance is another sign. A student who normally gets good grades and is suddenly failing classes, a good athlete who is kicked off the football team because of his attitude, or the parent who misses work often may be signaling a growing alcohol problem. Blackouts, where the drinker completely forgets what happened while drinking, are another key sign. Alcoholism is a progressive disease, so if a person drinks more than he or she used to and if relationships with family members are getting worse because of drinking, the person may indeed have a drinking problem.

Alcoholism is never cured, but it can be controlled. Once alcoholics stop drinking, many begin again. Some think that when they stop briefly, they have proven they can stop when they want to, so they really don't have a problem. But their lives remain a mess, and the problem drinking continues. Many experts believe that for alcoholism, as for other addictions, the key to lasting control is to consider oneself not as a recovered alcoholic but as a *recovering* alcoholic.

Treatment of Alcoholism

It's hard to get an alcoholic to seek help. Less than 10 percent of all problem drinkers are treated for their condition. Of those who are, higher success rates are reported for those who have been drinking for a shorter period of time and have somewhat stable lives, with a family and a good job. They have more to lose through their drinking. Private programs that handle this type of patient have reported 60 to 80 percent success rates. Public facilities with patients who have abused alcohol for long periods of time and who are unemployed, without family ties, have less than 20 percent recovery rates.

Once an alcoholic decides to get help, there are many options. The first for many is to seek help from a family doctor, who may prescribe treatment or recommend a hospital treatment center, a private rehabilitation program, or a self-help group.

The doctor will first administer an alcoholic evaluation test to determine how far the disease has progressed. The Michigan Screening test and the Mayo Clinic's Self-Administered Alcoholism Screening Test (SAAST) are written question-and-answer tests about the patient's drinking habits. The SAAST consists of thirty-seven questions such as, Do you have a drink now and then? Are you always able to stop drinking when you want to? Have you ever awakened the morning after some drinking the night before and found that you could not remember a part of the evening? Studies have found this test to be 95 percent effective in detecting alcoholics who are ill enough to warrant hospitalization. Blood tests may also be used and are up to 75 percent reliable in distinguishing people with alcohol abuse problems even if they have not had a drink in years.

Doctors have many treatment options for an alcoholic patient. One common approach is to create a chemical fence to prevent the alcoholic from drinking. *Disulfiram* (trade name *Antabuse*) was first used in 1948; today over 250,000 people in America are taking this prescribed drug. When a person taking Antabuse tries to drink, extremely unpleasant reactions occur, including vomiting, heart pounding, and hot flashes. These symptoms are caused by acetaldehyde, a product of alcohol metabolism that builds up when Antabuse blocks the reactions that normally remove it from the body. Antabuse does not work for all patients, and some doctors feel it should not be used for more than a month or two. Other milder chemical-fence drugs are also sometimes used.

The recovering alcoholic may need a special diet because alcoholism can cause severe malnutrition. High-protein, low-sugar diets are often suggested in frequent small meals to help regulate the blood sugar levels.

Another option is a treatment program. There are over 7,000 programs for alcohol abuse available in the United States, including inpatient hospital programs that normally run up to twenty-eight days, residential live-in programs that offer similar services in a nonhospital environment, and outpatient programs at night, consisting of therapy and educational sessions that allow the patient to carry on normal daily life. Alcohol treatment programs are a billion-dollar-a-year industry, and many insurance companies cover some or all of the costs.

Nearly all American programs require total abstinence from drinking. Other countries strive for drinking in moderation as the treatment goal. American experts believe that once an alcoholic begins with even one drink, eventually compulsive drinking will begin once again.

During the detoxification phase of the treatment, sedatives may be used to help the patient through withdrawal symptoms, which may last up to a few weeks. Once the alcoholic is completely sober, counseling and group therapy sessions follow to help the alcoholic relearn new behavior patterns. Some controversial approaches involve large doses of vitamins or steroid and hormone therapy, based on theories that alcoholism is due to vitamin deficiencies or an endocrine system defect.

Whatever the method used, nearly all programs rely heavily on Alcoholics Anonymous. This self-help group was formed in 1935 by two alcoholics. Today there are more than 63,000 local AA groups throughout the world, with an estimated 600,000 to one million American members. Members range through all age levels, from teenagers to senior citizens, and include more young people than ever before.

AA is a continuing source of support for recovering alcoholics. Members share their experiences and problems and often attend daily meetings with their AA group or with other local chapters. The buddy system encourages members to call another member for help whenever they feel the urge to drink.

AA is not a religious group. Many local groups, however, have a religious emphasis that turns off some potential members. The AA philosophy is based on the Twelve Steps, the first of which is the recognition that the individual is an alcoholic and is unable to control his or her condition. The alcoholic is urged to turn to a higher power for support. Some see this as God, others as the collective supportive group. AA is not a medical organization, although many AA groups also stress nutrition and other medical education.

AA claims that at least half of its members who attend regular meetings remain sober, but professionals point out that many do not stick with the program. Still, most experts feel that the emotional support that AA provides has made it an extremely effective tool in fighting alcoholism, especially when combined with other programs.

Further Reading

Barrymore, Drew. *Little Girl Lost*. New York: Pocket Books, 1990.

Berger, Gilda. *Addiction: Its Causes, Problems and Treatments*. New York: Franklin Watts, 1982.

Gold, Mark S., MD. *The Facts About Drugs and Alcohol*. New York: Bantam Books, 1986.

Hodgkinson, Liz. *Addictions: What they are—Why they happen—How to Help*.Wellingborough, England: Thorsons Publishing Group, 1986.

Hyde, Margaret O. *Alcohol: Uses and Abuses*. Hillside, N.J.: Enslow Publishers, 1988.

Ryerson, Eric. *When Your Parent Drinks Too Much*. New York: Facts on File, 1985.

US Dept. of Health and Human Services, National Institute on Alcohol Abuse and Alcoholism, *Communicating With Youth About Alcohol*. 1986.

Helpful Organizations

Alcoholics Anonymous
P.O. Box 459
Grand Central Station
New York, NY 10017

Al-Anon Family Groups
115 East 23rd St.
New York, NY 10010

Alcohol 24 Hour Line
1-800-242-6465

**National Clearing House for
Alcohol Information**
Box 2345
Rockville, MD 20852
(301) 468-2600

National Council on Alcoholism
733 Third Ave.
New York, NY 10017
1-800-NCA-CALL

**National Association for
Children of Alcoholics**
Suite 201
31706 Coast Highway
South Laguna, CA 92677
(714) 499-3889

Smoking

The first reports about the dangers of smoking tobacco were published in 1859, but cigarette smoking continued to increase in America and around the world. By 1949, 44 percent of all American adults smoked. That figure has been dropping steadily since the 1950s, however, and by the late 1980s less than 26 percent of American adults were smokers. In 1988, the American Lung Association estimated there were about 50 million American smokers, down from 54.5 million in 1986. But Americans still smoke about 600 billion cigarettes a year, and over three trillion cigarettes are smoked around the world every year.

The glamorous image of smoking on the Hollywood screen helped to shape people's attitudes toward the habit in America. Then, in 1964, the Surgeon General released a report on cigarette smoking that shocked the nation. The message was clear: Smoking kills.

The image of cigarette smoking began to change from a glamorous, socially accepted behavior to a habit that might have harmful health consequences. But it was still largely socially accepted. In the 1980s, public attitudes turned increasingly negative. This trend received a boost from the 1986 Surgeon General's report on the dangers of passive smoking. Many studies had demonstrated that those who did not smoke but who breathed the smoke of those who did had an increased likelihood of health problems, as well. Confrontations grew frequent (and occasionally violent) as smokers and nonsmokers debated their respective rights to smoke and to breathe clean air. The growing concern led to the passage of state laws restricting cigarette smoking in forty-two states by 1988. Smoking was barred or nonsmoking areas were required in various public places, such as restaurants, banks, stores, and workplaces. A 1988 federal law prohibited smoking on all airline flights lasting two hours or less, and in 1989 the restriction was extended to nearly all flights.

In May 1988 Surgeon General C. Everett Koop released another shocking report on cigarette smoking. The 618-page report declared that tobacco smoking is more than a simple habit—it is an addiction, just like heroin use. If you start smoking, you may not be able to give it up!

The tobacco industry and its supporters were predictably upset. They have long maintained that no cause-and-effect connection between cigarette smoking and health problems had been demonstrated. Brennan Moran, spokeswoman for the Tobacco Institute, responded to the Surgeon General's report: "The claims that smokers are 'addicts' defy common sense and contradict the fact that people quit smoking every day." Others were disturbed that Koop had declared smoking similar to illegal harmful drugs like heroin and cocaine.

The Surgeon General held firm. Cocaine and heroin kill about 6000 Americans each year, he pointed out. Alcohol-related deaths number 125,000. Smoking kills over 320,000 Americans each year! In 1986 the U.S. death tolls included 108,000 from smoking-related lung problems and 200,000 from smoking-related heart disease.

Shortly after the Surgeon General's report was published, a landmark court case awarded $400,000 in damages to Antonio Cipollone, whose wife Rose had died of lung cancer after smoking for forty years. Similar cases in the past had always held that the health consequences of smoking were the smoker's own responsibility. The verdict in the Cipollone case, however, stated that the tobacco company had violated a commitment to consumers to manufacture a safe product. Although cigarette packages now carry warnings of the health risks of smoking, Rose Cipollone had started smoking long before such warning notices were required; by the time the public became aware of the risks, she was already addicted.

What's in Cigarettes?

Cigarettes contain the leaves of the tobacco plant, which are burned and inhaled into the lungs. Two thousand different chemicals are released when the tobacco leaves burn, and all of these are inhaled into the smoker's body. Nicotine, carbon monoxide, and tar are the three main components of the tobacco leaves. All three contribute to the harmful health effects of cigarettes. Nicotine, however, is largely what gives the smoker satisfaction. It is also the chemical that causes the smoker to become addicted.

Nicotine is Addictive!

When the 1964 Surgeon General's report came out, the government officially considered smoking to be habituating for the first time, but it was not until 1988 that it was declared addictive. Nicotine meets all the standards of an addictive drug: it alters the mood, it produces tolerance and withdrawal symptoms, and its use becomes a compulsive behavior.

Nicotine is a stimulant. The average cigarette contains a little more than one milligram of nicotine, and nearly all of it reaches the bloodstream when a cigarette is smoked. Within thirty minutes, half of the nicotine is completely broken down; its effects begin to wear off, and craving for another cigarette begins. (Typically, nicotine-dependent smokers smoke a cigarette every half hour.)

The Surgeon General's report was based on many studies conducted over the years. In one study, for example, unmarked cigarettes containing high, medium, or low nicotine concentrations were given to smokers. Those who smoked the low-nicotine cigarettes took more puffs per cigarette, took less time between puffs, and smoked more cigarettes than those who had cigarettes with a higher nicotine concentration, even though none of them knew which was which. Smokers of low-nicotine cigarettes were also more apt to hold the smoke in longer and to smoke the cigarettes farther down than normal. Other studies showed that heroin addicts found cigarette smoking harder to quit than their heroin use. Significantly, there are many occasional drug and alcohol users, but very few occasional smokers.

Cigarette smoking is currently the most widely used method of self-administration of nicotine fixes. The drug can also be taken in other forms. It can be smoked in cigars or pipes, sniffed in the powdered form, snuff, or taken by mouth in the form of chewing tobacco. The example of professional ball players, who can be seen chewing and spitting on televised baseball games, has made chewing tobacco seem desirable to many young people. In fact, an estimated one out of twelve young males now use chewing tobacco.

Effects of Smoking

Generally people smoke because it makes them feel better, but not the first time it is tried. Typically, the first experience is not a pleasant one. It is not at all uncommon for the first-time smoker to cough, to feel dizzy and nauseated, and to break out in a sweat. The taste of the cigarette seems unpleasantly bitter. But is not long before smoking becomes a pleasurable activity. The body quickly builds up a tolerance to cigarette smoking, and with continued use dependence and addiction can follow.

Nicotine is a stimulant, but it also relaxes the body at the same time by affecting the nervous system. It takes about seven seconds for nicotine inhaled in cigarette smoke to reach the brain. That's twice as fast as for heroin injected into the bloodstream, and three times faster than alcohol taken in a drink on an empty stomach.

Many changes occur in the smoker's body during smoking. The heart speeds up fifteen to twenty-five beats per minute. Blood pressure rises ten to twenty points. The skin temperature drops as much as six degrees because circulation to the extremities is cut down. Muscles become relaxed, and the hypothalamus is stimulated to curb hunger for food. Smoking has been found to improve concentration and memory—many perform better on difficult tasks while smoking. It can also help reduce anxiety and increase tolerance of pain.

As in other addictions, researchers are finding a link between depression and smoking addiction. Nicotine's stimulating effects help smokers self-medicate their moods, and some smokers may use it as a way of avoiding or controlling feelings of depression and anxiety.

How Nicotine Works

Nicotine works by mimicking the hormone adrenaline and the neurotransmitter acetylcholine, which activates the brain's alarm system and causes the smoker to become alert. After only a few puffs, the nicotine level in the blood shoots up, the blood pressure rises, and the heartbeat accelerates. This speeding up of body processes cause the smoker to feel more alive and may help him or her to function better and think more clearly. At the same time, nicotine stimulates the production of endorphins, the body's natural opiates, producing a calming effect that helps push troubles aside.

Nicotine is not stored in the body, so a constant supply is needed to keep the positive effects going on. This is why smoking addicts enjoy the first cigarette of the day the most—because the body has gone all night without any nicotine.

Smoking can be a powerful addiction because it controls the smoker's mood and performance and can be self-administered at any time. Because the high is barely noticeable as compared to other drug highs, the smoker does not realize that the overall sense of well-being felt while smoking is anything out of the ordinary. And whereas the potential for overdose is great with narcotics, cigarette-related problems don't usually develop for twenty years or more. To the person smoking now, that seems far off and less urgent.

The Negative Side of Smoking

After a while, long-term smoking begins to produce some obvious negative effects on the body. Smokers begin to notice they get out of breath much more quickly, and they can't do many of the physical activities they used to. Many smokers develop a smoker's hack, a deep cough that never seems to go away. Smokers' teeth may become discolored, their breath is bad, and their clothes and hair smell of smoke.

Tobacco smoking brings far more serious risks than these, however. Cigarette smoking has been shown to cause bronchitis, emphysema, lung and other cancers, and heart disease. A person who smokes two packs a day, on the average, will die eight to nine years earlier than a nonsmoker. Up to 30 percent of all cancer deaths are smoking related, and 75 percent of all those who die from lung cancer are smokers! The lung cancer death rate for smokers is fifteen to twenty-five times greater than that for nonsmokers.

Even nonsmokers may have their health harmed by the smoke produced by the nicotine users. Studies have shown that nonsmoking spouses of smokers have higher rates of lung cancer than nonsmoking spouses of nonsmokers. Children raised in a household where someone smokes have a higher than average rate of colds and more serious respiratory ailments.

All told, more Americans die *every year* from smoking than have died in World War I, World War II, the Korean War, and the Vietnam War combined—over 320,000 people. Tobacco is the nation's leading cause of avoidable illness and death!

Women are always advised to quit smoking while they are pregnant. Studies have found that moderate-smoking mothers have nearly 30 percent more complications during pregnancy than nonsmoking mothers, and heavy smokers have 85 percent more complications. Some of the nicotine in the mother's bloodstream is transferred to the fetus, and the fetal heartbeat speeds up shortly after the mother takes a puff. The birth weight of children born to smoking mothers tends to be lower than normal.

Kicking the Habit

Eventually most smokers realize the risks of cigarette smoking are more than they bargained for. But cigarette smoking is not an easy habit to break because it is more than a habit for most; it is a real addiction. Nine out of ten smokers say they would quit smoking if there were an easy way to so.

Not only does smoking become a psychological crutch, but there are real physical withdrawal symptoms associated with quitting, as the body is deprived of its usual fix of nicotine. Although not everyone who tries to quit will experience such problems, many suffer from one or more of a number of narcoticlike withdrawal symptoms including breaking out in a cold sweat, suffering from insomnia, irritability, constipation, tension, anxiety, fatigue, difficulty in concentrating, and, of course, strong cravings to smoke. The pulse also slows down, blood pressure drops, and tingling in the hands and feet may develop. Although it takes quite a while for the tar and other chemicals to clear from the lungs (some damage is permanent), other physical changes occur much more quickly. More oxygen goes to the brain after smoking has stopped, and this sudden increase can cause occasional dizziness. Blood vessels that were once constricted because of a constant nicotine supply dilate, allowing the blood to flow more freely; this effect can cause tingling sensations. Even a cough can persist for a long time as the lungs try to clear out deposits.

One of the biggest psychological drawbacks for smokers trying to quit is the fact that they can expect to gain weight when they quit. On the average, smokers are seven pounds lighter than nonsmokers. Those who quit can quickly gain five to ten pounds.

Typically, ex-smokers feel the urge to eat carbohydrates and sweets. Carbohydrates seem to alleviate the tension and fatigue that comes with nicotine withdrawal. One theory is that the body thinks that starches and sugars supply the chemical that is missing during nicotine withdrawal.

Nicotine withdrawal symptoms may seem unbearable during the first day and may be even worse during the second to fourth days after quitting. After about a month, however, withdrawal symptoms will be mostly gone, but an intense craving for cigarettes can recur for years.

When these craving episodes arise, they usually last up to five minutes. The best way to deal with them is to distract oneself. Some doctors recommend snapping the wrist with a rubber band to make the brain forget about the craving. The harmless pain of the rubber band will force the brain to turn its attention away from craving. Most doctors recommend an increased amount of exercise to fight nicotine withdrawal, as well as a way to curb weight gain.

Although the Surgeon General's message that smoking can be addictive, just like heroin and cocaine, shocked and scared many people, Koop assured smokers that they should not be discouraged. For many smokers a genuine desire to quit and, if necessary, persistent and repeated attempts to quit may be all that is necessary. For others self-help materials, formal treatment programs, and nicotine replacement may be needed and should be readily available.

Quitting smoking is hard to do—three out of four people who quit smoking later start again. (This is the same relapse rate as for recovering alcoholics and heroin addicts.) But people do quit! Forty-three million Americans have quit for life. More than two-thirds of them quit on their own. The rest seek help from places like the American Cancer Society, the American Lung Association, or the American Heart Association, from private programs like SmokEnders, or from local hospital programs or church- or synagogue-sponsored programs. Most of the methods work as long as the person trying to quit really wants to quit and receives a lot of encouragement. However, no one program or method is right for everyone.

Many studies have been conducted to examine what types of smokers have the best chances of quitting for life. Some studies have found that it is harder for women to kick the habit. In one Finnish study, those who were more likely to quit had smoked for shorter periods of time. They smoked fewer cigarettes each day, were better educated, were employed, married, slept more, and were more satisfied with life.

An American study conducted by Geoffrey Kabat and Ernest Wynder of the American Health Foundation showed similar results. The researchers also noted that white people have a greater probability of quitting than blacks, and Jewish smokers are more likely to quit than non-Jewish smokers.

Surprisingly the researchers found that both light smokers and heavy smokers were more inclined to quit than moderate smokers. Those who smoke one to ten cigarettes a day are less likely to become addicted, so that finding was not too surprising. Perhaps the heavy smokers quit more successfully than moderate smokers because heavy smokers would have more obvious smoking-related symptoms like shortness of breath and heavy coughing, giving them added incentive.

The study also revealed a link between the amount of time that elapsed from waking up to having the first cigarette of the day and the probability of quitting. For those who lit up within fifteen minutes after waking, the quit rate was only a little more than one in three, but for those who waited an hour or more, the quit rate was over 60 percent. The amount of time waited before the first cigarette of the day seems to be a strong indication of habituation or the severity of the addiction.

One study found that the foods a smoker eats can affect the desire to smoke. Chicken, eggs, peanuts, and cheeses raise the acidity level in the body. Raw vegetables, however, such as beans, carrots, and tomatoes, as well as fruits like strawberries and bananas, make the body fluids more alkaline. The higher the acidity level, the faster nicotine will be excreted in the urine. The study suggested that eating raw vegetables may cause nicotine to stay in the body longer, thereby reducing the desire to smoke.

Prevention

It's hard to quit smoking, so the best treatment is prevention—convincing people not to start in the first place.

Most smokers start young. Studies have found that nearly all smokers begin before the age of twenty. In recent years, nearly every age group except teenagers has cut down significantly on cigarette smoking. Teenage smoking is increasing. Each day 2,000 teenage girls start smoking. One study found that 40 percent of high school students had tried smoking cigarettes, and one out of five smoked every day. Forty-three states have laws restricting the sale of tobacco products to minors, but for the most part, according to Surgeon General C. Everett Koop, they are not properly enforced.

Unlike adult smokers, teenagers can start and stop smoking many times. Health educators, therefore, approach teenage smoking from both prevention and intervention angles. Researchers find that the more teenagers smoke, the greater the chance that they will become hooked for the rest of their lives. One study declared that 90 percent of all teens who smoked twenty cigarettes over the span of an entire year became regular smokers!

Researchers find many similarities in young smokers. Those whose friends smoke usually start before teens whose friends don't smoke. Young teenagers want to belong, and it's hard to say no. Often parents' attitudes toward smoking have a lot to do with whether or not a person will start smoking. Teenagers whose parents smoke or consider it acceptable are more likely to smoke themselves.

Teens who do not do too well in school are more likely to begin smoking. For some young people smoking is a form of rebellion. Most beginning smokers are more rebellious than nonsmokers of the same age.

101

Nearly all who take up smoking think that they can quit whenever they want to. They don't think that they are starting something that they will be doing the rest of their lives. They also don't believe that they will get lung cancer and heart and respiratory problems that older smokers get.

Some smoke for confidence, others to relieve unhappy feelings. Some like the way it makes them feel. Others are swept up in the image portrayed by the tobacco industry's multibillion-dollar advertising campaigns that portray smokers as successful and attractive.

Some researchers feel that smoking may be an inherited tendency, as is believed to be the case for other addictions. Those who are addicted to nicotine are often addicted to other substances as well. One study found that 96 percent of all heavy smokers were heavy coffee drinkers, too. Ads for liquor or cigarettes often show people drinking as well as smoking, because many smokers light up while they drink.

By educating the public about the hazards of tobacco, health officials hope to help smokers quit, as well as help young people decide not to get hooked in the first place. The Surgeon General has made it clear that he hopes America will be tobacco free by the year 2000.

That goal probably will not be reached. Tobacco has been an important American and world commodity for too long. Christopher Columbus found the Indians smoking tobacco leaves and brought the plant back to Spain with him. In less than fifty years, tobacco was being smoked all over Europe. By the seventeenth century, it was being used throughout the world. The American Revolution was largely financed by tobacco sales. Over the years, many countries have tried to limit tobacco use. At one time, Japanese smokers could be imprisoned. In Germany, Persia, Russia, and Turkey, anyone who smoked could be punished with death! Still, all these measures did not stop people from smoking. Even today, with all the known health risks tobacco can bring, people still choose to smoke.

Treatment of Nicotine Addiction

For years, doctors have been telling patients to quit smoking. With the Surgeon General's warnings, patients may see an even greater effort by their doctors to get them to quit. At the 1988 annual meeting of the American College of Physicians, doctors were urged to take a renewed interest in the smoking behavior of their patients. Doctors are now more apt to ask patients if they smoke and whether they are interested in quitting. If the patient says no, the doctor will often provide a pamphlet and offer help if the patient should decide to quit.

For those who want to stop smoking, the doctor may set up a specific date when the patient will try to quit and then schedule a follow-up visit one to two weeks later. Studies have found that those who have a follow-up visit are twice as likely to be successful in kicking the habit.

Family doctors may recommend nicotine gum to those who are heavily addicted. Those who smoke more than a pack a day, those who smoke within half an hour after they wake up, those who continue even when they are sick, and those who have experienced withdrawal symptoms when they tried to quit in the past may be helped by this approach. The gum is carried everywhere and used whenever the urge to smoke arises, but after six to twelve months of use it should be tapered off.

Each month 100,000 people use Nicorette (the brand name of nicotine gum) for the first time. One million Americans are said to have been successful in kicking the habit with Nicorette. But a troubling new trend is emerging. Some people are becoming addicted to the nicotine gum, and many are using it as a substitute for smoking because of all the restrictions against smoking in public places. Even though Nicorette is available only with a prescription, many find ways around this technicality.

Researchers are currently developing other ways to deliver replacement nicotine, in the form of a nasal spray and of stick-on patches that administer tiny doses of the drug through the skin. The high-blood-pressure drug clonidine, used in narcotic addiction programs, is also showing some promise in helping smokers kick the nicotine habit.

One of the most popular approaches utilizes behavior modification, based on the idea that smoking is a learned behavior. The smoker learns to replace smoking with alternative activities, and the learning process is reinforced by various rewards for good behavior and punishments for smoking. Limits are set on how many cigarettes the smoker is allowed to have each day. This limit is gradually lowered. Such programs stress physical exercise and also rely heavily on relaxation exercises.

Over-the-counter aids that may be used as substitute crutches for the smoker trying to quit include nicotine-free cigarettes, smoking-deterrent tablets and gums, and filters that help wean smokers off cigarettes. Success rates vary, but some of the aids on the market have been found by the FDA to be ineffective and possibly unsafe.

Organizations like the American Cancer Society and the American Lung Association offer self-help programs, with free booklets containing useful suggestions. For example, the smoker trying to quit is given tips on avoiding temptation:

1. Get rid of everything that has to do with smoking—ashtrays, lighters, and most of all cigarettes!
2. When you feel the urge to smoke, breathe in deeply, hold it for a second or two, then breathe out very slowly. This rhythmic breathing will give the sensation of smoking, without smoking.
3. Chew sugarless gum, or eat fruit, nuts, or unbuttered popcorn when you feel the urge to smoke. Drink lots of water. Oral substitutes are often necessary to stop the craving for smoking. But beware of sweet and spicy foods, which can increase the desire for smoking. Eating smaller meals throughout the

day will help maintain constant sugar levels in the body, which will help fight nicotine craving.

4. Exercise is important to help relieve the tension that comes with withdrawal.

5. Keep your hands and thoughts busy with hobbies or routine tasks to distract yourself before craving begins.

6. Avoid places that you associate with smoking, as well as drinking alcohol and caffeine, which are often associated with smoking.

Each year millions of smokers try quitting in November on the American Cancer Society's annual Great American Smokeout. An average of twenty million smokers cut down or try to quit every year on that day. Only about one in five, or less, stick with it, however, and quit for good. The goal of the annual event is to provide smokers who want to quit with a supportive atmosphere and an excuse to try and kick the habit; almost half of all smokers at least cut down for that day.

Group programs include many AA-type clinics in which smokers help each other overcome their addiction through group support. Such programs are sponsored by the American Cancer Society and the American Lung Association, as well as local schools, churches, and synagogues. Private programs are also available. One of the most widely known is SmokEnders, which utilizes a behavior modification approach.

Many find psychotherapy valuable in helping overcome the desire to smoke. Some find hypnosis effective. Programs that teach the smoker to use self-hypnosis can help some people.

Whatever method is chosen, it will work only if the smoker really wants to quit. Stress or anxiety can set the stage for a relapse; being around smokers can also be a great temptation. Even one cigarette can start a quitter smoking again. In one study, 50 percent of a group of smokers who had quit returned to smoking in the first month after smoking a single cigarette. By the end of a year, 83 percent were smoking again. But if a smoker is unsuccessful in staying off cigarettes, the defeat may not be permanent. Evidence shows that the more attempts that are made, the greater are the chances of quitting for life. And the longer a person stays away from smoking, the better the chances of quitting for life.

Further Reading

Berger, Gilda. *Addiction: Its Causes, Problems, and Treatments.* New York: Franklin, Watts, 1982.

Burton, Dee. *The American Cancer Society's Freshstart 21 Days to Stop Smoking.* New York: Pocket Books, 1986.

Byrne, Gregory. "Nicotine Likened to Cocaine, Heroin." *Science,* May 27, 1988, p. 1143.

E. Jeanne. *The Twelve Steps for Smokers.* Center City, Minnesota: Hazelden Foundation, 1984.

Freifeld, Karen. Smoke-Free Forever. *Health,* November 1987, pp. 12–13.

Gorman, Christine. "Why it's so hard to quit smoking." *Time,* May 30, 1988, p. 56.

Hodgkinson, Liz. *Addictions: What they are—Why they happen—How to Help.* Wellingborough, England: Thorsons Publishing Group, 1986.

Holzman, David. "Potent from the First Ancient Puff." *Insight,* May 8, 1989, pp. 50–51.

Rogers, Jacquelyn. *You Can Stop.* New York: Pocket Books, 1983.

Stop Smoking Program Guide. American Cancer Society.

"We are vending addiction to our children." *The Saturday Evening Post,* July/August 1989, p. 100.

Helpful Organizations

For free pamphlets contact your local:

American Cancer Society
American Lung Association
(800) 4-CANCER (for the location of
a nearby medical center program)

SmokEnders
50 Washington Street
Norwalk, CT 06854
(800) 243-5614

Caffeine

Caffeine is the most widely used drug in the world. It is completely legal, cheap, and—most important—readily available. But it is a mind-altering stimulant, and it can be addictive. Many people can't start their day without a dose of caffeine. It is estimated that one out of five people in America may be addicted to this drug—and they are not all adults. Many parents are either not aware or don't care that every day their children are eating and drinking foods that contain this drug.

Coffee is the most common source of caffeine. In recent years, however, coffee drinking has decreased in the United States. A little more than half of all Americans drink coffee, compared to three out of four twenty-five years ago. Nearly one in five people now drink decaffeinated coffee, versus less than one in twenty-five a generation ago. Still, billions of cups of coffee are drunk every year in the United States, and the average person drinks nearly thirty gallons of coffee a year.

Coffee is not the only source of caffeine. Americans drink more than thirty-five gallons of soft drinks a year, and most of the leading brands contain caffeine. One would expect cola drinks to contain caffeine, but others, like Mountain Dew and Sunkist Orange Soda, have this drug in them as well. (Mountain Dew has more caffeine than the leading colas!) Caffeine is found in tea and chocolate, too. It is also an ingredient in some headache tablets, antacids, cough formulas, diuretics (water pills), and allergy pills.

Caffeine belongs to a group of chemical compounds called methylxanthines. It is a natural substance that can be found in more than sixty different types of plants, including coffee beans, kola nuts, cocoa beans, and tea leaves. When it is extracted, its white crystals look like sugar, except that instead of being sweet, they have a bitter taste.

The caffeine found in various food products is chemically the same, but different sources contain different amounts of the drug. Coffee beans have the most caffeine, but the amounts of it in different types of coffee beans vary. The way the coffee is prepared also has a lot to do with the amount of caffeine. A cup of brewed coffee can contain up to 180 milligrams of caffeine, while a cup of instant coffee may have only 50 or 60 mg. Teas and colas have considerably less, usually about 30 to 60 mg of caffeine, and chocolate bars around 10 to 20 mg.

History of Caffeine

According to legend, coffee originated about 1500 years ago. One day an Arab goat herder in ancient Abyssinia (now Ethiopia) noticed his goats were particularly active after munching on the red beans of a wild bush. The goat herder decided to taste the beans himself, and soon he was dancing around, filled with energy.

Meanwhile, a holy man saw the goat herder and his goats dancing about, and when he learned about the beans, he prayed to Mohammed about the power of the beans. In a dream, Mohammed told the holy man to boil the beans in water and drink the concoction so that he would be able to stay up for long hours and pray. This drink was called kahwa after the Arabic word for wine.

During the Middle Ages, coffee was brought to Europe, where it was used as a medicine for measles and smallpox. In the eighteenth century, coffee was so popular that people drank it in coffee houses as much as they drank liquor in taverns.

Quantities of Caffeine in Various Substances

brewed coffee	about 100 mg (40-180 mg)
instant coffee	about 65 mg (30-120 mg)
decaffeinated coffee	about 3 mg (1-5 mg)
tea	about 50 mg (20-90 mg)
colas	about 50 mg (30-70 mg)
hot cocoa	about 5 mg (2-20 mg)
chocolate milk	about 5 mg (2-7 mg)
baking chocolate, 1 oz.	35 mg
semisweet chocolate, 1 oz.	about 20 mg (5-35 mg)
milk chocolate, 1 oz.	about 6 mg (1-15 mg)
Vivarin	200 mg
NoDoz	100 mg
Excedrin	65 mg
Anacin	32 mg

Note: For beverages the portion size is 1 cup. For medications the amount of caffeine is equivalent to one pill. Ranges in parentheses indicate variations due to differences in brand or method of preparation.

Over the years, doctors noticed coffee's possible side effects, such as headaches and insomnia, but people didn't listen. They liked the taste of coffee and the way it made them feel. Many countries tried to limit coffee use, and at various times coffee drinkers were looked on as bad or common people. At one time in the seventeenth century in Moslem countries, anyone who drank coffee in public could be condemned to death!

Tea drinking has an even older history. According to Chinese legend, tea has been drunk for almost 5000 years. It was brought to Europe from China and Japan by Dutch traders in 1610, and by 1650 it was carried to the American colonies.

Kola nuts are native to tropical Africa and were taken to many parts of South America for cultivation. The kola nut was chewed by natives to fight off hunger and tiredness. In some places, the nuts have been considered so important that they were used as money.

Effects of Caffeine

Most people drink coffee, tea, or cola drinks to give them a little pep or lift in the morning or when they are getting tired. Caffeine is absorbed through the intestines into the bloodstream and travels to every part of the body. About a half hour after swallowing it, the user begins to feel the effects.

For those who are not used to taking caffeine, the effects will be more pronounced. After about an hour, the blood pressure rises slightly. The heart rate decreases at first, then increases. Breathing speeds up. Adrenaline levels rise. The metabolic rate speeds up. The blood vessels around the heart and in the hands and feet dilate (open wider), but the blood vessels in the brain constrict (narrow). These effects are less noticeable in those who take caffeine on a regular basis because the body builds up a tolerance to the drug.

After about five hours, half of the caffeine in an adult body is metabolized. The amount of time it takes for the body to break down half of the amount of any drug is called its *half-life*. For pregnant women, caffeine's half-life is twice as long as for a normal adult. For children six to ten years old, it is only about half as long, but the half-life of caffeine in newborn babies is over four days!

There is still some controversy concerning caffeine addiction. Most scientists feel the drug is mildly physically addictive, while some believe it is only psychologically addictive. It is listed with other forms of addiction in the International Classification of Diseases.

Many studies on the effects of caffeine have been conducted. In one early study of three hundred women, three-fourths of the subjects felt the need for a cup of coffee first thing in the morning. For many of them, missing that morning cup often resulted in a headache that incapacitated them for hours.

In another study, coffee drinkers and nondrinkers were given unmarked packages of instant coffee to be taken first thing in the morning. Some contained super-caffeinated coffee (300 mg), some 150 mg of regular coffee, and some decaffeinated coffee. The subjects kept a log of how they felt after taking their morning coffee for a week and a half. The researchers found that the heavy coffee drinkers who drank decaffeinated coffee felt sleepy and irritable both before and after they drank the beverage. Heavy drinkers who got the 300-mg coffee felt good after their first cup of coffee. Coffee nondrinkers who got caffeinated coffee felt uncomfortable and fidgety, and sometimes nauseous. The researchers were able to confirm the real physical effects of caffeine on regular users and nonusers as well.

Evidence suggests that a tolerance builds up after using coffee for an extended time. People often drink more coffee as they get older—forty- to fifty-year-olds drink the most coffee.

Scientists feel that 350 mg of caffeine a day is enough to cause the body to build up a tolerance. It is believed that 600 mg a day can lead to physical dependence and addiction, although some think dependence can arise with less. The dose that produces tolerance is equivalent to the amount in about

113

five cups of instant coffee a day, not counting other sources of caffeine—well within the level taken by many.

In children, the amount needed for addiction is much lower because their body weights are smaller and because caffeine is metabolized more quickly in children than in adults. Thus, a child who has three cola drinks and two chocolate bars a day is actually consuming an amount of caffeine equivalent to an adult who drinks eight cups of coffee—well above the level considered to be addictive.

Stopping caffeine use produces real withdrawal symptoms in heavy users who have become addicted to it. The most common withdrawal symptoms are headaches, irritability, sleepiness, sluggishness, and nausea. (These are the same symptoms that may occur with large doses of caffeine— 600 mg or more. In addition, many users find that they crash or feel tired after the caffeine high wears off.) A heavy caffeine user who decides to stop taking the drug can avoid the worst of the withdrawal symptoms by cutting down the daily dose gradually, rather than stopping all at once.

Many different claims have been made about caffeine —both good and bad. Because it is a stimulant and affects the central nervous system, caffeine fights off drowsiness. It is also thought to quicken the reaction time and to allow the user to think more clearly.

Over the last fifteen years, caffeine has been implicated in over one hundred diseases and disorders, such as diabetes, cirrhosis of the liver, ulcers, hypertension, gout, cancers of the kidney, bladder, and pancreas, increased cholesterol levels, heart disease, fibrous breast cysts, birth defects, miscarriages, and underweight babies. However, for every claim about caffeine's possible negative effects there is an equal amount of research in which no connection to caffeine was found.

Because of the conflicting reports, most doctors are reluctant to tell their patients to stop drinking coffee or tea (as long as it is in moderation), with a few exceptions. Pregnant women are urged to at least cut down to one cup of coffee a day. When a pregnant mother drinks caffeine, the drug crosses over the placenta to the fetus. Since the half-life of caffeine in the fetus may be five days or more, the baby can be exposed to high levels of caffeine for long periods of time. Caffeine has been shown to prevent laboratory animal fetal cells from repairing DNA damage. Also, since caffeine causes blood vessels to constrict, the fetus could be getting a lower oxygen supply, which may cause a lower birth weight. These effects have not been proven in humans, but studies have shown that when pregnant mothers drink one to ten cups of coffee a day, their newborn babies may experience caffeine withdrawal symptoms of rapid heartbeat and increased breathing rate. Caffeine can also pass into breast milk. Babies of nursing mothers who take caffeine have been found to suffer from insomnia and crankiness.

The long-term effects of caffeine are difficult to study because the drug produces different reactions in different people in different situations. Caffeine makes some people tired, for example, instead of pepping them up. The time of day the caffeine is taken and what other medications, drugs, or foods are taken along with it all have an effect. It is also hard to measure how much caffeine a person takes in, considering the different caffeine levels in different brands of coffee and cola drinks.

Because of these variations, studies have concluded that caffeine raises blood pressure levels, lowers them, or produces no change at all. Some research suggests that caffeine lowers the body's sugar level; thus, taking a lot of caffeine over long periods of time could cause nervousness, headaches, and tiredness, just as experienced by those with low blood sugar problems. But other researchers found that caffeine raises the blood sugar level. The same conflicting results have been found for the heartbeat, respiration, metabolic rate, and cholesterol levels.

Caffeine can relieve headaches by constricting blood vessels to the brain and scalp, but it can also cause headaches by agitating the nervous system.

Caffeine withdrawal produces headaches because the constricted blood vessels dilate in a rebound effect.

Large doses of caffeine (around 600 mg) can produce insomnia, headaches, irritability, and nervousness, as well as faster or irregular heartbeat. Excessive use of caffeine for some time can cause trembling, depression, anxiety, insomnia, nervousness, flushing of the face, and heart palpitations. It's also possible for *caffeinism*, an anxiety-type disorder due to low-level poisoning, to develop with continued large doses of caffeine.

Caffeine is a drug, and it can be fatal if the user takes too much of it. However, to overdose on caffeine, one would have to take in 5 to 10 *grams* of caffeine, which would be equivalent to 200 cans of cola, 125 cups of tea, or 75 cups of coffee—all within a short period of time. Cases of caffeine overdose have been reported, however. Some people take super pep pills that contain more than 350 mg of caffeine each. Some types, now outlawed, contained over 500 mg of caffeine combined with other types of stimulants. More than a dozen caffeine overdose deaths due to these pep pills have been reported in recent years.

The Biochemistry of Caffeine Stimulation and Addiction

Caffeine works by blocking the action of a natural chemical sedative in the body called *adenosine*. Adenosine plays a role in getting the brain ready for sleep. Like all neurochemicals, adenosine attaches to specific receptor sites in the brain. When it does so, it reduces the cell's activity. Caffeine has a similar structure to adenosine and attaches to the adenosine receptor sites. When these receptors are tied up by caffeine, adenosine cannot produce its sedating effects, and the brain cell continues to fire.

There are adenosine receptors in various parts of the body. Caffeine affects many different body systems because it can attach to all of these adenosine sites. Scientists are working to produce caffeinelike drugs to improve alertness without many of the side effects that come with caffeine. These future drugs will affect only the brain receptors and not the other systems of the body.

According to Richard Wurtman at MIT, withdrawal symptoms occur because of the way the body builds up a tolerance with continued use of caffeine. With prolonged caffeine use, more receptor sites for adenosine are produced within the blood vessels of the brain, so that there is more of a chance that adenosine will reach some receptors, permitting the body to function normally. But when caffeine intake is stopped suddenly, more receptor sites pick up adenosine, and the blood vessels become dilated, causing the nerve endings in the blood vessel walls to fire. The result is a headache. Caffeine withdrawal headaches are more likely to affect those who normally get headaches.

Many people suffer from caffeine addiction and withdrawal without knowing it. Many pain-killers contain caffeine, and often chronic headache sufferers fall into a vicious cycle when they take them. At first, the pain-killer relieves a headache, but then a new headache may start because the body builds up a dependence on the caffeine in the pills.

After a few days without caffeine intake, the receptor sites return to normal and the withdrawal symptoms go away. Tapering off caffeine slowly is the best way to prevent withdrawal.

People who are addicted to caffeine are often addicted to other things as well. In one study, nearly all heavy smokers (96 percent) were heavy coffee drinkers as well (or users of other forms of caffeine). Nearly half of those who smoked more than a pack of cigarettes a day drank more than six cups of coffee each day.

As more research into the connections between addiction and depression is done, scientists are beginning to see that many drug users seek out addictive substances to relieve their depressive moods. This seems to be the case with

117

caffeine. Researchers believe that many are unconsciously or consciously taking caffeine to pep themselves up when they are feeling down or in low spirits. Stimulants actually used to be given to treat depression until the 1950s, when antidepressant drugs came into use, so this idea may not be so farfetched.

Unlike most other addictive substances, caffeine is a part of most people's normal lives. Its use is not illegal, nor is it restricted by age—even though the amounts of cola drinks and chocolate consumed by children are often above the addictive levels. Some experts believe that this nonchalant attitude toward caffeine addiction needs to be reexamined.

Further Reading

Alcohol, Tobacco, Caffeine & Pregnancy. Phoenix, Arizona: Do It Now, 1985.

Berger, Gilda. *Addiction: Its Causes, Problems, and Treatments.* New York: Franklin Watts, 1982.

Eisenberg, Steve. "Looking for the Perfect Brew." *Science News,* April 16, 1988, pp. 252–253.

Gilbert, Richard. *Caffeine: The Most Popular Stimulant.* New York: Chelsea House, 1986.

Grady, Denise. "Don't Get Jittery Over Caffeine." *Discover,* July, 1986, pp. 73–79.

Hodgkinson, Liz. *Addictions: What they are—Why they happen—How to Help.* Wellingborough, England: Thorsons Publishing Group, 1986.

McCarthy, Paul. "Strong Coffee, Weak Babies." *American Health,* October, 1986.

Food

We all have to eat. If we didn't, our bodies wouldn't get the nutrients we need to continue functioning, and we would die. Most people enjoy eating. It's one of life's simple pleasures. But for some people food becomes the center of attention. They can't stop thinking about food. It becomes an obsession and a compulsion, and some would say an addiction.

There are several ways a person can be said to be addicted to food. All of them involve a constant focus on eating. The most obvious food addict is a person who compulsively overeats. But others, who suffer from *anorexia nervosa,* are equally obsessed with food but force themselves *not* to eat. *Bulimia* is still another food addiction, in which a person goes on food binges, eating uncontrollably, and then purges out the food. All of these conditions can have quite serious consequences.

Food addiction can distort the way a person looks at himself or herself. It can strain relationships with friends and family and eventually break them. It can cause people to lose their jobs and their ability to deal with life. Severe health problems, hospitalization, and even death can result from food addictions.

Food disorders are a growing problem in America. The number of overweight children in the United States has gone up more than 50 percent in the last twenty years. It is estimated that there are between ten and eighty million overweight people in this country today. The higher figure is nearly one-third of the whole U.S. population! (Overweight is defined by most experts as weighing 10 percent more than the average for a particular age/height/sex/body frame group. *Obese* is defined as 20 to 30 percent or more over the average for the group.) Anorexia and bulimia seem to be growing problems as well. Twelve percent of women between the ages of thirteen and twenty-one suffer from either anorexia or bulimia, and 6 percent of those cases are fatal.

Morbidly obese is the term doctors use to describe patients who are more than one hundred pounds above the average for their weight class. Evidence has shown that morbidly obese patients are at a greater risk from many disorders, including heart disease, strokes, high blood pressure, and diabetes. Obese people generally do not live as long as people of normal weight. One study found the average life span to be ten years less for obese individuals.

Anorexia nervosa can cause severe problems due to a lack of the vital nutrients needed to keep the body going. Twenty percent of anorexic cases are fatal! The popular singer Karen Carpenter was one of the victims. Many bulimics believe that bulimia is not as dangerous as anorexia. But chronically induced vomiting can damage the teeth and cause serious internal damage to body systems; eventually heart problems are also likely if the condition persists.

It's easy to see how food can gain such importance in a person's life that it can become a psychological addition. It is a basic need that is one of the first to be filled when we are young. A baby cries when it is hungry, and food calms the child as well as the parents' nerves. As the child grows, sweets and treats are often rewards for good behavior. They are often a consolation, too, when things don't go well. When we are older, meals become an important time for social interaction—with families at dinnertime or friends in the school cafeteria; they can be an important thing we share together. Some of the most important business deals and decisions are made over lunch. And what is more romantic than a candlelit dinner?

Traditionally, eating disorders were thought to be due to psychological problems. But research is providing insights that point to biochemical causes. The problem may be much more than a psychological one; it could be a physically addictive one.

The Biochemistry of Food Addiction

A good meal is usually a pleasurable experience. Some brain researchers believe that the pleasant feelings a hot fudge sundae brings are actually a natural high produced by chemicals in the brain. They believe that certain foods, as well as other pleasures in life (like watching a good movie, listening to music we enjoy, or exercising), stimulate the production of natural morphinelike pain-killers, the endorphins, which are produced by the body to help relieve discomfort and stress.

Research by psychologist Elliott Blass at Johns Hopkins University has suggested that sweets may stimulate endorphin production. In an experiment with rats, he found that sugar has a morphinelike calming effect. Naltrexone, a drug that blocks the production of endorphins, seems to block the calming effects of sugar as well.

Endorphins are produced when we are subject to stress or when we have not eaten in a while. They help to restore the body's energy reserves by making us desire protein and fats. Indeed, in laboratory tests, rats that were injected with morphine ate more protein and fat, but when injected with a drug that blocks morphine, they did not have this desire.

Some experts believe that in eating disorders something goes wrong with the natural balance of endorphin production, and the person becomes addicted to the endorphins produced. Applying this theory to bulimics, eating binges may be the result of a chemical imbalance. But each eating binge then further contributes to the imbalance. Research at the University of Wisconsin in Madison indicates that bulimic patients do indeed have higher levels of endorphins in their blood than normal people. Jeffrey Jonas, at Fair Oaks

Hospital in Summit, New Jersey, has reported success in treating bulimic patients with drugs that block endorphin production.

Other researchers are studying anorexia nervosa. Mary Ann Marrazzi and Elliot Luby at Wayne State University in Detroit believe that psychological factors cause young women to be concerned about their weight and to begin severe and strict diets. Then, after about three months, their bodies actually become addicted to dieting. The addiction becomes so strong that patients will continue dieting even when they know they are seriously ill.

Many in the medical field disagree with the endorphin theory. They argue that if it were true, then anyone who dieted for a long time could become anorexic, but this just isn't the case, and the condition, although growing, is still found mainly in young women.

The Wayne State researchers answer this objection with the theory that anorexics are genetically susceptible to having an unbalanced opioid system. Our bodies are designed so that the opiatelike substances (endorphins) are produced to protect against starvation by helping the body to conserve energy and resources. Endorphin production causes a coupled response. That means that it prompts two different body responses and that one occurs when the other one does. Endorphins cause a lowering of the body's metabolic activity to the bare minimum needed to survive. (Many anorexics find their heartbeat slows down, and in most cases so much weight is lost that they no longer have their monthly menstrual cycle. When faced with starvation, the body will stop all unnecessary functions that are not directly needed to survive.) At the same time, endorphins are designed to stimulate the craving for food, so that the person will eat more and not starve. In anorexic-prone people, something goes wrong, and the responses become uncoupled. The body becomes addicted to the opioids (the body's natural opiates), and the craving for food disappears.

In testing this theory, the researchers treated eight anorexic patients who were hospitalized for their condition with the opiate-blocking drug

123

naltrexone. Six of the patients gained weight while on the drug; one was back to her normal weight and began menstruating again.

Critics of the study say that the results were meaningless. Nine out of ten anorexic patients in a good hospital program will gain weight while in the program. Although many recover from anorexia, there is no known quick cure.

The very nature of an anorexic patient makes it difficult to determine whether this drug or other treatments are effective because it is extremely hard to get anorexics to continue treatment once they leave the hospital. When they start gaining weight, they may become frightened and go back to dieting. Like other addicts, they can recover but are never cured of their addiction. They have to avoid dieting for the rest of their lives.

Further support for the idea that anorexia is an addiction is furnished by observations that one-fourth to one-half of all anorexics are also addicted to substances like alcohol, cocaine, or other drugs. This cross-addiction is a typical addictive pattern.

Wayne State researcher Mary Ann Marrazzi discovered that rats and mice react differently to an injection of morphine. The mouse becomes hyperactive and anorexic, while the rat becomes hungry and tired. Normal people react like the rat when they receive morphine or when their bodies produce natural endorphins. It is a pleasurable experience, but it does not permanently alter their normal eating patterns. But the mouse's reaction is similar to that of an anorexic-prone human.

Researchers are also examining obesity and compulsive overeating in terms of physical and biochemical causes. Evidence suggests that obese people have lower levels of endorphins in their blood. They may be overeating to produce a feeling of well-being, and a cycle develops in which they become addicted to overeating in order to compensate for the lower endorphin levels. Indeed, tests using naloxone, a drug used to treat morphine and heroin overdoses by blocking opiates, have shown that humans do eat less when injected with this endorphin blocker. In experiments at the Eating Disorders Clinic at the University of Michigan, ten normal-weight women were given a nonaddictive opiatelike drug, butorphanol. When they were offered various snack foods, these women preferred sweet-tasting foods and those high in fats. But when they were given naloxone along with the synthetic opiate, they tended to turn down chocolate bars and cookies in favor of snacks with fewer fat calories.

It would appear that pleasure and food intake are very closely related. When we're hungry, almost anything smells delicious. Even water tastes good when we're thirsty. If the endorphin theories are correct, a major advance has been made in our understanding of how people experience pleasure and why some become addicted to these experiences.

Other researchers are exploring the role of other brain chemicals in appetite and eating patterns. Sarah Leibowitz, a neurobiologist at New York's Rockefeller University, believes that at different times we experience hunger or a craving for different food types. For example, sometimes we're in the mood for a pizza, and other times a thick juicy steak is what we crave. Endorphins and other neurotransmitters control our desire for carbohydrates, fats, and proteins—the three main food groups. But at the same time, the types of food we eat can affect the production of these neurochemicals.

When we drastically change our eating habits, such as going on a severe diet, the brain chemistry is altered. Sarah Leibowitz observed that experimental rats tend to overeat later to compensate when one of their feedings is skipped. She and other researchers believe that dieting techniques such as skipping meals or cutting out one of the food types (carbohydrates or fats) can cause confusing signals that change the balance of brain chemicals.

Each of the neurochemicals seems to affect certain specific food types. Dopamine, for example, has the opposite effect to endorphins—it suppresses the desire for protein. Norepinephrine and neuropeptide Y stimulate the desire for carbohydrates. In one Rockefeller University experiment, a rat injected with neuropeptide Y ate as much in four hours as it would normally consume in two days. Rats injected with the neuropeptide and then allowed to choose among carbohydrate, fat, or protein meals always chose the carbohydrates.

Neuropeptide Y normally builds up when rats are without food for a while, for example, before the first meal of the day. This reaction seems to be a means of regulating blood sugar levels through hunger for carbohydrates. But if the rats receive continual injections of neuropeptide Y, chronic overeating and obesity result. Researchers believe that in humans, cycles of surging neurochemicals may set up an addictive condition causing overeating, which may lead to obesity. In the case of bulimics, binge eating and purging may produce surges of the peptide in the brain, or an imbalance could trigger abnormal eating patterns.

Other brain chemicals also seem to play a role in appetite. The neurotransmitter serotonin inhibits the desire for carbohydrates. Richard Wurtman, a neurochemist at MIT, believes that when we eat carbohydrates, serotonin production in the body goes up, so that the next time we eat, we won't eat as many carbohydrates. Maybe this theory explains why you might not feel in the mood for pizza for lunch if you had a big spaghetti dinner the night before.

Low levels of serotonin and norepinephrine in the brain have been linked to severe depression. Some antidepressant drugs seem to work by increasing serotonin levels in the body. Richard and Judith Wurtman and Harris R. Lieberman at MIT suggest that some obese people may eat carbohydrates to keep from getting depressed. They found that people who typically overeat mostly carbohydrates feel less depressed than those who overeat other types of snacks. These carbohydrate cravers could account for up to half of all obese people. Carbohydrate cravers may thus be unconsciously trying to medicate themselves for low serotonin levels with high-carbohydrate foods. These foods raise the serotonin levels and improve the eaters' spirits. As carbohydrate snacking is continually used as a way of feeling better, an addictive eating pattern may develop.

Researchers have found that antidepressant drugs such as fluoxetine, which raise serotonin levels, also reduce the tendency to overeat under stress. The drugs not only relieve depression but also decrease carbohydrate snacking as well, and the patients lose weight. Patients who responded to fluoxetine said they ate less because after a few bites they no longer had the urge to eat. Fluoxetine has also shown promising results in treating bulimia.

Other Theories on Eating Disorders

Other factors that might cause food disorders are also being explored. Brain researchers who are convinced of physical and biochemical causes of food disorders point to a part of the brain called the hypothalamus as the area where appetite control takes place. In laboratory tests, rats whose hypothalamuses were injected with drugs that stimulate hunger went on eating binges, while those injected with appetite-suppressant drugs stopped eating. In other tests, rats with a damaged hypothalamus began to eat continuously—they had no appetite control. Although their eating habits eventually tapered off, they remained heavier than normal. Damage to a different part of the hypothalamus produced too much appetite control—the animals ate much less than normal.

The control centers in the hypothalamus monitor the levels of various chemicals in the blood and respond to changes in them. One of the chemicals that may play a key role in appetite control is insulin, a hormone produced by the pancreas. Insulin is secreted after a meal, as the blood sugar level rises, and it prompts liver cells to take up sugar molecules and store them away as the animal starch glycogen. This hormone may also affect the appetite controls that tell the body when to feel full. In one experiment conducted by researchers at the University of Washington, baboons were injected with insulin. After the injection, the baboons ate less and lost weight. Researchers also found that a specially bred strain of obese rats had almost no insulin in their brains, whereas a strain of lean rats had rather high levels of insulin.

Other studies found that obese patients' red blood cells had lower levels of sodium-potassium ATPase, an important enzyme that helps regulate the body's energy consumption. Perhaps an enzyme imbalance is responsible for the overefficient metabolism in obese people that causes less energy to be consumed to carry on normal functions.

Studies have shown a high correlation between a low metabolic rate and a tendency to gain weight. Some people can eat and eat and never gain weight, while others eat just a fraction of that amount and put on pounds. A study of obese children found that a lower metabolism had already been established by the time the child was three months old. Fidgeting has also been found to be related to higher metabolic rates and a lower weight; people who remain active while resting are less likely to be overweight. Other studies have concluded that after a period of dieting the body's metabolic rate slows down as a natural defense against starvation. This finding explains why many overweight people hit a plateau when dieting and can't seem to lose any more weight no matter what they do.

Some people appear to have a hereditary ability to store fat more readily than others. This characteristic was an advantage for early humans, who had to face cold environments and times when food was scarce. Stored fat is good insulation against cold, and a starving body can draw on its fat reserves to keep going. With modern living conditions, however, the fat-storing trait can be a disadvantage.

Many studies have confirmed the idea of hereditary factors in eating disorders. The weight of adopted children tends to correspond better to that of their natural parents than to that of their adopted parents. In studies of twins, it is twice as likely for both of a pair of identical twins (who come from the same fertilized egg and therefore have exactly the same genetic material)

128

to be obese than it is for nonidentical twins (who have only half of their hereditary information in common).

Researchers like Jules Hirsch at Rockefeller University believe that within ten years we will know how the obesity gene works and that we will better understand the biological factors that regulate body fat and find ways to manipulate them with drugs.

Still, many believe that food disorders are mostly psychological. Indeed, most of the treatment available to people with food disorders is approached from this standpoint. Many specialists believe that these disorders are a learned behavior, and to cure them one has to change that behavior. Studies have found, for example, that in homes where food is the center of attention and easily available, children are more likely to become obese.

Some psychologists believe that people with eating problems have an oral fixation and never developed normal eating habits. They feel this fixation stems from being fed too much or too little as a baby. The conflicting values that parents and society express can also produce emotional confusion about eating and lead to problems. All around us, the media, advertising, and people's attitudes tell us thin is in. Slim spells success; fat spells loneliness. And yet, most advertising is for food products, and eating is also perceived as a happy experience and a sign of prosperity. Parents urge us to eat up so that we can grow up healthy and strong. But children who eat too much are chided with "You'll get fat if you keep this up."

These conflicting values can cause confusion particularly in adolescents, who are experiencing new changes in their bodies and are more concerned about who they are and how they look to the world. Most bulimics and anorexics, for example, have a distorted view of the way they look. They may feel they are fat, even when they may be grossly underweight. Obese people often have bad feelings about their size and develop emotional stress because they think there is nothing they can do to change. This attitude, of course, only contributes to gaining weight, as they eat more to compensate for their feelings.

Food Addiction?

So are eating disorders true addictions? Are they physical or psychological addictions? Are they emotional and psychological ways of coping with stress and depression? Are they the result of biochemical processes and imbalances? The specialists do not fully agree about the causes.

At a New York Academy of Sciences conference, experts pointed out that obesity and other food disorders should not be viewed as single disorders with single causes. There are many theories, and some are more useful than others in helping to treat people with food disorders. It does seem evident, however, that the trend in the future will be to focus on the biochemical aspects as we gain a greater understanding of how the body and its inner processes work. Thus, future treatments for eating disorders will undoubtedly involve various drug treatments to counter chemical imbalances and break addictive cycles. These breakthroughs will bring better results in the fight against food addictions.

Treatment of Eating Disorders

There are a number of resources for helping people with eating disorders. Unfortunately, many are reluctant to seek help. Most morbidly obese people, for example, have seriously tried dieting, but nearly 95 percent gain back most, if not all, of the weight they took off. In the case of anorexia nervosa and bulimia, admitting a problem is one of the biggest hurdles to overcome. By the time most anorexics seek help, they are already in need of medical attention.

Most of the current treatment available for eating disorders views the problem as a psychological one. Anorexia nervosa and bulimia patients (or their worried parents) can seek help at hospitals or clinics with eating disorder

130

programs. Such agencies as the American Anorexia/Bulimia Association, Inc., the Anorexia Nervosa and Related Disorders (ANAD), and the National Anorexic Aid Society (NAAS) can help in finding the right program for a person in need.

Some eating disorder programs involve hospitalization until the patient is nutritionally stable. Others work on an outpatient basis. Current treatments involve individual psychotherapy, family counseling, and nutritional therapy, as well as the use of antidepressant drugs in cases when the patients are so depressed they don't want to be helped. A treatment team is usually made of doctors, psychiatrists, social workers, and nurses.

The first step in treatment of anorexia is to get the patient to gain weight. Behavior modification is used in many hospital programs. A behavioral contract may be set up, in which privileges, such as being allowed to leave the hospital for an outing, are granted when weight is gained. Bulimics are not allowed to binge on food or to purge food in most programs. Rewards and penalties are also used in many bulimia treatment programs.

Individual psychotherapy is needed to help patients understand what is happening to their bodies, to help them discover some of the psychological reasons for their abnormal eating habits, and to aid them in overcoming the destructive behavior patterns.

Like other addictive diseases, anorexia and bulimia affect not just the victim but the entire family as well. Therefore, family therapy is also important to help the family provide support for the anorexic and to better equip them to deal with the problem.

Hospital programs usually last from one to six months, and during that time proper eating habits are encouraged so that the patient can lead a normal life. Patients learn ways of coping with daily stresses and worries without turning to abnormal eating patterns. Emphasis is placed on building self-esteem. Good programs offer extensive outpatient counseling after the hospital program ends because eating disorders are never really cured. It is a continual struggle. Typically, more than a third of the patients in a program go right back to the same habits. Another third revert somewhat, and only one-third maintain proper eating habits for an extended time after treatment.

The best place to start fighting obesity is with children. We form many of our eating patterns as children, and research has shown that fat-cell development begins in childhood. Although the number of overweight children in America has gone up in the last twenty years, health officials are concerned with America's obsession with dieting. Polls have revealed that nearly one-third of all eight-year-old girls have dieted. Half of America's nine-year-old girls have been on a diet, and 80 percent of the ten- and eleven-year-olds diet! Dieting can be dangerous for anyone if proper nutrition is not part of that diet. But for children, dieting can create especially serious problems. Children's bodies are still growing, and without proper nutrition irreversible damage can be done. What America should realize is that dieting is not the answer. The American Academy of Pediatrics urges exercise as the answer, not dieting. Society's attitudes need to change. Almost two-thirds of girls of all ages polled felt they were overweight, but less than one in five really was.

Nevertheless, obesity is a problem for many people. Treatment usually involves three steps: diet, exercise, and psychological support.

Dieting usually means cutting down on the amount of food taken in. Many diets cut down selectively, with less carbohydrates and more protein than usual, or more carbohydrates and less protein, or some other variation. Many experts believe, however, that the best type of diet is to eat the same proper portions of food, just less of each. With fewer total calories taken in, the body consumes more of the food for present needs and may start to draw on its reserves of stored fat. The result is a loss of weight.

Unfortunately, losing weight is only part of the battle. And difficult as it may be, it is far easier than keeping the weight off. Diet alone is usually not enough to accomplish it. Most people who diet gain back all or most of the weight they lost.

Exercise is an important part of losing weight and keeping it off. It helps get the body in better shape and reduces the overall proportion of fat in the body by producing more muscle. Counseling is an important part of all good programs, too. Many weight problems involve emotional problems that cause the person to overeat. Alternatives to overcoming depression, anxiety, and stress are explored so that food will not be the cure the compulsive eater turns to.

If endorphins are indeed involved in food addictions, then alternative pleasurable experiences that produce endorphins are a way of substituting for those that would have been generated by eating. Listening to music you enjoy, engaging in a hobby that is fun and exciting, or watching a good movie can produce endorphins to help ward off food cravings.

Sometimes hypnosis is useful in weight reduction. Under hypnosis, the patient is given suggestions on sticking to goals of weight loss and encouraged to build up self-esteem and confidence. Self-hypnosis, where the subject suggests these goals, is also helpful for some people.

Some programs involve behavior modification. Their basic idea is that overeating is a behavior that is learned. Thus, it can be unlearned and another behavior substituted in its place. The learning process can be reinforced by negative associations—for example, harmless but uncomfortable electric shocks received by the patients when they look at pictures of food. Eventually they associate food with the negative stimuli and do not eat as much.

Others respond better to positive reinforcement. Dieters are rewarded with praise or nonfood rewards when they lose weight or resist temptation.

When losing weight is a life-and-death situation and no treatments seem to work, some resort to drastic approaches. One last resort is an operation on the stomach called vertical-banded gastroplasty, in which a pouch is made surgically at the opening of the stomach. Only the pouch fills with food, not the whole stomach. An inflatable balloon that is swallowed into the stomach is another alternative that is being explored. The balloon keeps the stomach feeling full, and less food is eaten.

Liposuction is another alternative. Fat is sucked out of specific areas in the body by plastic surgeons. There are some doubts about the safety of this procedure, however, and the results can sometimes be unsightly.

In almost any newspaper or magazine, you can find ads for "miracle" weight-loss pills. The only miracle they perform is to collect money from gullible customers. Most doctors do not favor medications as a means of weight reduction because any drugs potent enough to be effective in weight-loss programs tend to build up tolerance and even addiction in the users. Eventually, safe and effective weight-loss pills will become available. Researchers today are working on pills to suppress the appetite, drugs to help the body burn off calories by utilizing more energy, and drugs that decrease absorption of fat by the body.

There are many groups, such as Weight Watchers and Overeaters Anonymous, to help people break their compulsive eating addictions. These groups help those with weight problems to understand about proper nutrition and exercise, in addition to providing support as the compulsive eaters attempt to change their life-styles. Unlike the self-help programs for other addictions, participation in weight-loss programs usually is not free. Some of them also provide specially designed diet foods to furnish a controlled calorie intake—another expense for the recovering food addict.

Further Reading

B, Bill. *Maintenance for Compulsive Overeaters.* Irvine, CA: CompCare, 1986.

Berger, Gilda. *Addiction: Its Causes, Problems, and Treatments.* New York: Franklin Watts, 1982.

Hodgkinson, Liz. *Addictions: What they are—Why they happen—How to Help.* Wellingborough, England: Thorsons Publishing Group, 1986.

Compulsive Overeaters Guide, Vol III: Overweight Teenagers. Penngrove, CA: Visually Handicapped Inspiration Library, 1984.

L, Elizabeth. *Twelve Steps for Overeaters.* New York: Harper & Row, 1988.

Latimer, Jane E. *Reflections on Recovery: Freedom from Bulimia and Compulsive Overeating.* Boulder, CO: Living Quest, 1984.

Helpful Organizations

American Anorexia/Bulimia Association, Inc.
[local chapters provide information and referrals to doctors and clinics specializing in eating disorders]

American Anorexia Nervosa Association, Inc.
133 Cedar Lane
Teaneck, NJ 07666

Anorexia Nervosa and Associated Disorders (ANAD)
Suite 2020
550 Frontage Road
Northfield, IL 60093
or
P.O. Box 7
Highland Park, IL 60035

The Center for the Study of Anorexia and Bulimia
One West Ninth Street
New York, NY 10024
(212) 595-3449

Eating Disorders Hotline
(800) 624-2268
[information and referrals]

Food Addiction Hotline
(800) USA-0088
[information about bulimia and compulsive overeating]

National Anorexic Aid Society, Inc. (NAAS)
P.O. Box 29461
Columbus, OH 43229

National Association to Aid Fat Americans (NAAFA, Inc.)
P.O. Box 43
Bellerose, NY 11426
(516) 352-3120

Obesity Foundation
5600 S. Quebec Street, Suite 310B
Englewood, CO 80111

Overeaters Anonymous
P.O. Box 92870
Los Angeles, CA 90017
(213) 386-8789

Adrenaline

We tend to think of stress as a bad thing, and often it is. But some stress can be a healthy thing for the body, helping to keep it toned up and ready for that extra push needed in an emergency. Putting out that extra effort and meeting an emergency successfully can be exciting, but it is not something the average person would want to do very often. Some people, though, seem to get addicted to stress and seek out situations that will set their fight or flight hormones flowing. These adrenaline junkies have discovered a number of different ways to get their natural drug.

Work

In our society, people who work hard are the ones who are praised. Teachers tell you in school that if you work hard, you will have a better chance of being a good student. At a job, the hard workers are usually the ones who are noticed and promoted.

There is an old saying, "No one ever died of hard work." It may not be true. People who need to work all the time are called Type A personalities. Those who are able to work hard when they are working, but can relax when they are not, are called Type B personalities. Type A people typically live stress-filled lives, and they are more likely to suffer from headaches, ulcers, and heart attacks. In addition, these workaholics are very bad at maintaining

137

meaningful relationships, can't handle criticism, and are often very narrow minded.

A hard worker is not necessarily a workaholic. It is more a question of the role work plays in the person's life, rather than how much time is spent working.

Psychologists say that workaholics are similar to alcoholics in many ways. Workaholics use their drive to always be working as an escape from facing themselves or their lives. They may work to avoid becoming close to people. Another motivation is the high they feel while they are working. When they aren't working, they feel anxious and uptight, angry and agitated. Work helps to fill an emptiness they feel inside.

In addition to the psychological explanations, there may be biochemical reasons for work addiction. Workaholics live under constant stress, racing to meet deadlines that they may have created artificially. Under stress, the adrenal glands pour out the fight or flight hormones, adrenaline (also called epinephrine) and norepinephrine. These chemicals are stimulants, toning up the body and exciting the mind (although they can leave a person feeling burned out if the stress continues too long). The workaholic may become addicted to this stimulation and unconsciously seek stressful situations to keep the stimulants flowing.

Workaholics are not necessarily effective workers. Even though they are working all the time, often they are so disorganized that they do not get any more done than a person who puts in a regular day's work. They are often rigid and unable to change their way of thinking. They feel the need to be in a position of control, and they are very bad at delegating tasks to other people— they'd much rather do it themselves and know it will be done right. Their feelings of insecurity and low self-esteem make them constantly try to prove something. They need continual praise for their work. Often workaholics suffer bouts of depression.

Hard workers, on the other hand, are people whose lives are not turned upside down because of their work. They work hard because that are trying to achieve a specific goal. When they are not working, they still can enjoy themselves.

Between school, homework, sports, chores, and other activities, you might feel sometimes you never have a moment to yourself. Could you be developing into a workaholic? Maybe you need to take time out now and then to think about what is really important to you. There is nothing wrong with working hard. For most people, it is the only way to succeed in anything that is meaningful to them. Just make sure that you leave time for activities that are relaxing, too, and time for building relationships with other people. Learn to set realistic goals for yourself, and if you're a hard worker, you'll do fine.

Gambling

Gambling has sometimes been called the invisible disease because in most cases even the addict's closest friends, family, and spouse don't know about the problem until it is too late. Once families do find out, the stress and emotional strain can cause bitter marriage split-ups and financial catastrophes.

Not everyone who gambles becomes a compulsive gambler. For some, a weekend poker or bingo game or a visit to the racetrack or casino is a harmless pastime. Occasional gamblers may lose a little more than they thought they were going to, but they know their limits, and the fear of losing is enough to keep them from going in over their heads. But for some, gambling is exciting and stimulating. It is an escape from the monotony of reality. It becomes the only thing they think about and look forward to. Money lost on bets is not a loss; it's an investment. Soon they'll strike it big!

Most gamblers are men—some sources estimate up to 80 percent of compulsive gamblers are males. Generally males are more competitive and risk-taking than women. Many compulsive gamblers are extremely intelligent, and some are highly successful businessmen with a strong competitive drive. Their risk-taking drive helped them to become successful, but it can also become their downfall.

Compulsive gambling is a progressive problem. The person may start out occasionally dabbling in harmless activities but end up with an uncontrollable addiction. Many gamblers begin at a very early age. They might start out as children innocently shooting marbles or flipping baseball cards and then progress to playing pinball machines or video games and shooting pool. Obviously, not everyone who engages in these harmless games will become addicted to gambling, but when a person gets hooked, gambling will be a lifelong struggle. Addictive gambling patterns are often established by the time one is a teenager.

Most gamblers have low self-esteem. Some were abused as children or suffered the loss or absence of one of their parents. They are insecure about themselves and their lives, and they dream about that one big win that will bring them the good life. But when they do win, it's never enough. The money goes right back into more gambling. For some, the thrill of gambling provides the motivation to continue. Often, though, gamblers go on plunging because they have gotten into such much debt that moderate-size winnings don't begin to pay even what they owe. A vicious cycle develops as the gambler feels more and more driven to win back what he has lost.

Meanwhile, he continues secretly gambling away large amounts of money he cannot afford. He may mortgage his home, sell his car, spend his family's savings, even steal from his employers to support his habit. Unable to borrow from banks, he may borrow from underworld sources and—since nearly all gamblers lose more than they win—endanger his own life and his family.

Some psychologists believe that compulsive gamblers are trying to hurt themselves. They know they can never win, and they are punishing themselves because they feel worthless. The average gambler would not agree. He *knows* he's going to win this time! And meanwhile, he gets high on the thrill of betting, the excitement and suspense of waiting for the result.

Like the workaholic, the compulsive gambler is hooked on the stimulating effects of stress hormones and neurotransmitters and feels most alive when a bet is riding and his money is in jeopardy. The similarities to substance addiction are underlined by the frequent cross-addictions. Nearly a third of all compulsive gamblers suffer chemical dependencies on alcohol or drugs, and many are compulsive smokers. Like other addicts, many compulsive gamblers suffer bouts of severe depression.

Eventually, the stress and cycles of excitement and depression can cause the gambler's health to deteriorate. Anxiety and depression can lead to ulcers and heart problems.

The compulsive gambler's family and friends may try to help by continually bailing him out with loans or sympathy. This will be the last time, the gambler pleads. I know I can win back my losses this time . . . But the well-meaning attempts to help generally make the problem worse, and the gambler will not seek help for his addiction—or even admit he has a problem—until he hits bottom.

Unfortunately, there is no cure for compulsive gambling. As with other addictions, the compulsive gambler is faced with a lifelong struggle to control the urges to gamble. Mutual-help groups modeled on the Alcoholics Anonymous pattern may provide the needed support, but it is a difficult struggle.

There are so many different temptations to lure the compulsive gambler: racetracks, casinos, card games, sports games to bet on . . . . A gambler can even feel virtuous betting on a state lottery whose proceeds will partly go to support education, and church-sponsored bingo games imply approval of gambling. Compulsive gamblers don't really need this kind of rationalization, though. If a betting opportunity is not available, they will make one, betting fortunes on the toss of a coin or something as silly as how long it takes a fly to land on a particular object.

Some states require that a telephone number for those who feel they may be addicted to gambling be posted at racetracks and at places where lottery tickets are purchased. Compulsive gambling hotlines are flooded with phone calls after major sports events like the Super Bowl or the World Series. Many people feel that sports betting is encouraged by the gambling jargon used by professional oddsmakers in the newspapers and on telecasts before a sports event. Help groups like Gamblers Anonymous say that if this type of commentary can't be banned outright, at least public service announcements about compulsive gambling should be presented to discourage betting on big sports events.

Older Americans are extremely vulnerable to the appeal of gambling. Retired, and perhaps alone after the death of a spouse, these older people are left with free time that they may not know how to fill. Millions go to casinos in Las Vegas or Atlantic City each year. The average person who takes the bus to Atlantic City's casinos goes eighteen times a year. Often these bus trips are practically free. Nearly the entire ticket price is refunded in coins for slot machines or coupons for meals and drinks when they get off the bus. This added incentive can be dangerous for the elderly person with nothing to do—or for anyone else, for that matter.

Senior Days at the racetracks are another pitfall for the elderly. Almost no one goes to the racetrack just to watch the horses—most spend at least a little more than they anticipated. Church bingo games can be dangerous, too, because they appear so innocent. Many senior citizens play several times a week, and it is not uncommon to lose $10, $20, even $50 a night.

As more and more states adopt lotteries, many find themselves pursuing that elusive giant jackpot. Someone has to win, and I have the same chance as anyone else!

With all the forms of gambling available, it is hard not to dabble just a little. But you cannot know in advance if you are one of the people whose dabbling may progress to an addiction.

If you find yourself gambling more often or think about placing bets or buying lottery tickets often during the day, or if you're gambling more than you can afford, gambling might be controlling your life. It's best to seek help as soon as possible, before gambling causes such great debts that your life begins to fall apart.

Risk-Taking

Why do some people enjoy the thrill of a roller coaster or thrive on horror movies that S-C-A-R-E them silly? Why do people skydive, climb up the sides of buildings, hang glide, or drag race? Recently, risk-taking behavior has become the focus of attention for scientists, sociologists, and law enforcement officers for a number of reasons. Teen deaths are one. Another is the AIDS crisis. Many AIDS cases develop in people who engage in high-risk activities, particularly intravenous drug use and promiscuous, unprotected sexual activity.

In 1987, medical professionals from many different specialties met to discuss this issue at a conference sponsored by the National Institute of Mental Health. At this Self-Regulation and Risk-Taking Behavior conference, psychologists, sociologists, brain researchers, and many other specialists examined all kinds of risk-taking behaviors from skydiving to drunk driving, robbery, and murder. The experts came to the conclusion that the American culture is in the middle of an epidemic of violent and self-destructive risk-taking behavior.

Young people seem to take the most risks in life. Since 1960, the death rate has declined for every age group except that from age ten to the mid-twenties. This distressing statistic has led to a number of studies by the government and private organizations to discover why so many young people are dying. Three-fourths of all deaths in this age group result from accidents, suicides, and homicides. Psychologists see these deaths mostly as the result of reckless behavior in high-risk activities, like drugs, speeding, and drinking while driving.

There is a lot of debate about why people are willing to endanger their lives by taking apparently foolish risks. It just isn't rational, which is why some call risk-taking behavior motivated irrationality. But what motivates thrill seekers to be irrational?

Various psychological factors have been found to shape those who need to take chances in dangerous situations. Peer pressure and an inability to judge risky situations correctly, as well as various hormonal changes that peak during adolescence and in the early twenties, are the most obvious factors behind risk-taking behavior. Some also say the high-action influence of television and movies nurtures a desire for thrills in an otherwise ordinary life.

Some psychologists believe we are brought up to view danger and risk as exciting and positive experiences. When parents toss children up in the air, only to catch them safely in their arms, they are actually encouraging dangerous behavior.

Some believe that certain people are born with a predisposition toward taking risks and seeking thrills and new experiences. These hereditary differences seem to have a biochemical basis. Using sensation-seeking scales that measure a person's desire to seek out new experiences that might involve physical and/or emotional risks, psychologists have found a correlation between this behavior and biochemical and neurophysiological changes within the body.

One of the most primitive brain activities is the response to physical danger. Adrenaline floods into the blood vessels, the heart races, and attention becomes fixed and focused—all to help one to fight or to flee from danger. Roller coasters and activities like skydiving are safe simulations of physical

144

danger, which activate the danger mechanisms in the brain. For some this heightened state is an exciting rush. Others find the adrenaline-sparked sensations extremely unpleasant. Researchers believe that thrill seekers get hooked on the biochemical changes that occur in the brain during dangerous intense experience.

According to Marvin Zuckerman, a psychologist at the University of Delaware, a chemical imbalance in the brain causes this need for intense physical excitement. Thrill seekers have lower than normal levels of monoamine oxidase, a brain enzyme that has been linked with several forms of depression. (Monoamine oxidase breaks down the neurotransmitters that promote sensations of euphoria.) Another brain chemical, dopamine beta-hydroxylase (DBH) is found in low concentrations in people who are manic and in sensation seekers, as well. (BH converts dopamine to another neurotransmitter, noradrenaline.) Thrill seekers also have higher levels of male sex hormones that are linked to aggressive behavior. Zuckerman believes that a craving for thrills may be due to faulty control mechanisms that fail to keep these brain chemicals in balance.

Psychologist Seymour Epstein at the University of Massachusetts believes that the total absorption and complete concentration that comes with intense experiences blocks out any problems or inner conflicts the thrill seeker might be experiencing. Thus, thrill seeking becomes a way of self-medication for underlying problems.

Another theory, held by Frank Farley at the University of Wisconsin, is that thrill seekers have a lower level of arousal than normal. Physical danger activates the reticular activating system at the base of the brain, which causes the entire body to become alert and excited and the person to feel fresh and alive.

Other psychologists describe risk addiction in terms of *akrasia,* or lack of control. According to this concept, people generally make decisions in a logical manner, but when the mind becomes weakened, other outside forces can greatly alter a decision, making the person choose a risky behavior when there are safer alternatives available. One theory is that certain bits of information are stored in the mind in ways that prevent their being utilized properly in making decisions. Young people who smoke, for example, are not doing so based on an informed choice, as tobacco manufacturers claim. They are aware of the risks, but this information is shaded and distorted. They may overestimate the number of adults and friends who smoke and underestimate the potential risks.

Sometimes taking risks can be a form of protest, of taking control of one's life. Young people may do risky things to show their independence from their parents. Risk-taking may be done with the intent of hurting oneself, as punishment for something the person feels guilty about.

Risk-taking can also be the result of misprocessed information. In one study, subjects were asked which they would rather do, invest $500 in a low-risk situation or invest $50 in a definite loss situation. Most chose to risk the $500. But when people were told that they could insure their $500 with a $50 premium, they chose the insurance—even though that $50 premium was a guaranteed loss. Sometimes it's all in how a question is posed. Reference points by which we judge how risky particular actions are vary by age and sex, as well as individual and cultural factors.

American culture is filled with mixed messages. People are told not to take chances, but then they watch television shows like *Miami Vice* that are filled with action, adventure, and violence. For some people, watching such fantasies is enough to satisfy cravings for excitement. But risk-taking urges are all too often unleashed in real life, too, in the form of destructive activities. Homicides in America, for example, have doubled in the last twenty years, and the rate is ten times as high as in most other industrialized countries.

Yet taking risks is a normal part of living. If we didn't take risks, life would be boring, with few outlets for curiosity, creativity, or personal growth. You have to take risks to ask someone out on a date, to get a job, or to seek

146

permission to do something of which you're not sure your parents will approve. The key thing to learn is just how much to risk and how to realistically predict the amount of peril involved in an action. Everyone has different risk tolerances—different levels that they can handle. Just because your friend goes skydiving doesn't mean it is a risk you are willing to take.

Taking risks is normal and healthy, as long as we understand what is involved and are able to weigh the benefits against the possible consequences. Those addicted to risk-taking behavior cannot weigh the benefits and consequences properly. The desire to seek out things that are exciting and thrilling—at any cost—may eventually cost the risk addict's life.

Treatment of Adrenaline Addiction

One type of adrenaline addiction, compulsive gambling, has an established treatment. Compulsive gamblers can seek therapy from a psychologist, who will help them gain control over their lives by helping to raise their self-esteem. Gamblers can also seek help from a money management center to aid them in getting their financial situation back in order. But since the urge to gamble may be a lifelong struggle, long-term treatment is essential.

Gamblers Anonymous is an AA-type support group program for compulsive gamblers. Many members need to attend meetings every day to keep themselves free from gambling. (Although most groups do not meet every day, there are so many chapters that by going to different groups, the addict can find a meeting in session every day.)

As with other Anonymous groups, members read the group's beliefs and goals and share their problems and concerns. Members remain anonymous, and last names are never used. Gamblers Anonymous believes that once a gambler, always a gambler. Like the recovering alcoholic who can never have even one drink, recovering gamblers can never gamble again or else they might not be able to stop.

Through peer support, gamblers learn to be responsible for their actions. Often arrangements are made so that the gambler's money is regulated by the spouse or some other concerned person, and the gambler never has any spare money. Paychecks may be arranged to go directly toward specific payments so that the gambler will not be tempted to gamble away rent money and car payments.

Further Reading

Work

Minirth, Frank B. et al. *The Workaholic and His Family.* Grand Rapids, Mich.: Baker Book House, 1981.

Gambling

What is G.A.? Center City, Minn.: Hazelden Foundation, 1985.

Lesieur, Henry. *The Chase: The Compulsive Gambler.* Rochester, Vt.: Schenkman Books, 1984.

Welles, Chris. "America's Gambling Fever." *Business Week,* April 4, 1989, pp. 112–120.

Risk-Taking

Goleman, Daniel. "Why Do People Crave the Experience?" *The New York Times,* August 2, 1988.

Weiss, Rick. "How Dare We?" *Science News,* July 25, 1987, pp. 57–59.

Helpful Organizations

Gamblers Anonymous
National Service Office
P.O. Box 17173
Los Angeles, CA 90017
(213) 386-8789

The National Council on
Compulsive Gambling
444 W. 56th Street
Room 3207S
New York, NY 10019
(212) 765-3833

Lesser-Known Addictions

Experts today also recognize a number of other compulsive behaviors. These lesser-known addictions include exercise, love and sex, television and shopping. Each of these normal activities can be abused, leading to a situation where a person becomes "addicted."

The key to all of these addictions is the narrow focus on a particular kind of behavior, which becomes the center of the addict's life. He or she begins to live for the next "fix." A growing number of studies suggest that there are deep similarities between substance addictions and compulsive behaviors in the biochemistry of the brain. Neurotransmitters and their receptors seem to play key roles in both types of addictions. Compulsive exercisers, shoppers and television watchers; those who flit from one love affair or conquest to another—all seem to use their behavior of choice in much the same way that substance addicts indulge in their drug of choice.

Exercise

America is caught up in a fitness craze. For most people this has been one of the better fads to come along. Millions of people are running or joining aerobic exercise classes, for example. These people are helping to get their bodies in better physical condition, which is making them healthier and stronger.

Exercise has another important benefit as well. It is a good way to release stress and anxiety. Many people find exercise makes their minds sharper and helps them relax during the day and sleep better at night. Often people just feel good after exercising. The "runner's high" is an expression now used to describe the good feeling that vigorous exercise can produce.

Some psychologists feel that the runner's high is like a natural drug high. In fact, researchers have found that strenuous exercise results in the production of endorphins. These natural pain-killers help a person to continue the physical exertions, temporarily ignoring the aches and pains of minor muscle strains or bruises. Meanwhile, the flood of endorphins in the brain also produces feelings of well-being.

Some people find so many benefits from their exercise program that it becomes a compulsive activity, the focus of their lives. They have become addicted to exercise.

Why do exerciseaholics keep exercising, even through the dead of winter? In addition to enjoying the "high" feeling, many who are used to exercising daily find that they feel miserable if they stop. They feel depressed and have trouble falling asleep at night. During the day, they are filled with anxiety and are unhappy with themselves, their bodies, and their lives. They suffer withdrawal symptoms from the sudden cutback in endorphin production.

Maybe you're thinking that addiction to something healthy like exercise isn't such a bad thing. In 1976 psychiatrist William Glaser wrote a book called *Positive Addiction*, about people becoming addicted to running. He acknowledged that many people run to help cope with life's problems and relieve stress—the same reasons people use drugs. But drugs destroy the body; running builds up the body and the mind as well. So even if running is addictive, what's wrong with it? Nothing, Glaser claimed. It's a positive addiction.

It wasn't long, though, before people began questioning this view. Some people still do not believe that exercise addiction really exists; others say that all addictions—even to positive things like exercise—have serious negative aspects. Most exerciseaholics push themselves to the limits, often to the point of injury. They may keep on running (or biking or aerobic dancing) in spite of injuries to muscles, tendons, or bones. Then the injuries get worse, sometimes disabling.

In addition to the endorphin effects, some experts see psychological explanations for exercise addiction. For most of us, there aren't many milestones in our daily lives. Not many things happen from day to day to show that we're making progress toward our goals. People who run every day typically set up daily goals for increased mileage or faster times, and each day brings measurable progress and achievements. The time of running or exercising becomes a highlight of the day. It provides something to look forward to, something that helps give identity and meaning to life. If they can't exercise, they can't measure success any more, and life becomes dull and monotonous.

Many injured exerciseaholics seek the help of a doctor to heal so that they can continue exercising. But solving the injury isn't really solving the problem. Exercise addiction, like other addictions, disrupts people's lives and affects the way they deal with jobs or school, family and friends. Instead of being enriched by exercising, their lives have become narrowed to this single preoccupation and source of pleasure.

The key to making regular exercise a positive part of life is moderation. Wise exercisers don't push themselves so hard that they invite injuries. It's also a good idea not to rely solely on one form of exercise or activity. Running, swimming, biking, racquetball, and other forms of exercise use different sets of muscles, and it is best not to overwork any of them.

As in all forms of addiction, the key is not to allow one activity to become the only outlet for coping with life's problems. It's best to become involved

152

in several activities, so that if you are unable to continue one of them, it won't be the end of the world.

Love and Sex

"Addicted to love . . . " The words of contemporary singer Robert Palmer's popular song are all too true for many Americans.

Love addiction and sex addiction are viewed as two different problems, although they are related and often go together. The love addict is constantly falling in love. A cycle of falling in and out of relationships develops. While the relationship is going on, everything is euphoric. But with each breakup, depression follows. This addiction typically occurs more in women than in men. The sex addict or "sexaholic" uses sex as a drug to relieve pain or deal with inner conflicts. The thrill of conquest and the excitement of secretive behavior that often goes with it are more important than the sex partner. Sexaholics are typically men.

Not everyone agrees that sex and love addiction are real disorders. There is some controversy as to whether they should be called addictive or whether a milder term like compulsive or impulsive would be more appropriate. The American Psychiatric Association currently says there is not enough evidence available to call these problems addictions. But the number of treatment programs that have been formed recently—and immediately filled to capacity—makes it obvious that sex addiction is a real problem for many Americans.

It is estimated that up to 6 percent of Americans are addicted to sex. Eight out of ten sex addicts who seek help are men, and nearly half are married. To the sexaholic, or "casanova" as they are sometimes called, sex becomes the most important thing in life. Although many sexaholics are promiscuous, the frequency of sexual activity is not the key signal of addiction; the important factor is the way sex is used. For the sexaholic, it is not a way of showing affection but, instead, a way of relieving depression, pain, and anxiety—a temporary escape from loneliness and low self-esteem. But sex doesn't necessarily make the addict happy. Many sexaholics are actually extremely depressed, and some are suicidal. Many are alcoholics or have other drug dependencies.

Casanovas compulsively seduce women (or men, if the sexaholic is a woman or a homosexual man) and then leave them to seek another conquest. Some are "swinging singles," going from one one-night-stand to the next; some are married but carry on a series of affairs. Sex addiction can also take the form of having one monogamous relationship after another. In each case, sex is used like a drug, and the compulsion can be destructive to the sexaholics and to their partners.

Up to half of all sex addicts were sexually abused as children. In many cases of male casanovas, the addict's father was not an integral part of the family, either because he wasn't there, he was always working, or he was an alcoholic. In these cases, the mother was overly involved in the child's life. Sometimes the mother would use the child as a surrogate husband and confide in her "little man." Since the child did not have a man around as a role model and his mother expected him to be "a man," he modeled his behavior after super-masculine characters on TV or in the movies and learned to treat women as objects.

Many sexaholics are proud of their conquests and feel no guilt about their actions. The addiction, however, can have disruptive and self-destructive effects. It can tear apart relationships and marriages, and sex addiction has been blamed in cases of child molestation and rape. The movies *Fatal Attraction* and *Looking for Mr. Goodbar* made it all too clear that there is a potential for violence in casual one-night affairs. With AIDS as a real and threatening problem, the promiscuous sexaholic also risks contracting this fatal disease. Sex addicts may recognize these problems but feel powerless against their compulsion.

154

The sex addiction treatment programs help people to learn that caring about others does not have to involve sex and that depression and insecurities can be relieved without having affairs.

Some casanovas are sex addicts, but some are love addicts. Love addicts go through cycles of falling deeply in love with someone and then, after winning their partner's affection, realize they were idealizing their lover and fall out of love, only to fall in love with someone else whom they idealize.

In her 1985 book *Women Who Love Too Much*, Robin Norwood stated that when these women speak about falling in love, they are really talking about being addicted to relationships. Love becomes a way of gaining control of one's own life and of the person in the relationship. This compulsion stems from a low self-esteem created by unfulfilled wants and needs while growing up because of parents who were too busy or were involved in alcohol or drugs.

Sometimes an addiction to love can lead to an obsession. *Fatal Attraction*, one of the hit movies of 1987, portrayed the darker side of romance. Although most people who are obsessed with love do not resort to violence, obsessive love is a common occurrence.

Most people long for things that they can someday attain. But some choose idealized goals that are unattainable, setting themselves up for relationships that will fail because they don't think they are worthy of relationships that will work. Yet they are convinced they cannot live without the object of their affections. Rejection threatens their very existence. In an effort to win their love object, they can make the other person's life and their own extremely miserable. Unlike the character in the movie, most obsessive lovers have such deep-seated feelings of low self-esteem that they are more likely to turn any violence toward themselves.

In addition to the psychological factors, there may be some biochemical causes of addiction to sex or love—an addiction to the feelings generated by being in love. Falling in love brings emotional and physical changes in the body. The heart rate speeds up, levels of lactic acid in the blood drop (making

155

one feel less tired and more energetic), and the levels of endorphins increase. Germ-fighting white blood cells become more effective, so that a person in love feels better and is actually healthier. Other brain neurotransmitters are also released in greater quantities. Romantic attraction increases the production of norepinephrine and dopamine in the brain, and these neurotransmitters enhance feelings of pleasure. Dopamine also affects the body's testosterone levels, increasing sexual desire in both sexes.

It is believed that increases of norepinephrine and dopamine are stimulated by another brain neurotransmitter, beta-phenylethylamine (PEA). Studies have shown that people in love have unusually high levels of PEA. This chemical has amphetaminelike effects, promoting feelings of euphoria and boundless energy. Researchers are still not sure whether we fall in love with a particular person because our brain produces more PEA, or whether falling in love causes an increase in beta-phenylethylamine production. When the love affair ends, though, PEA production drops abruptly, and there is an emotional crash.

For most people, falling in love is a rare occasion—often a once-in-a-lifetime experience. But some people are constantly falling in love and find themselves involved in one affair after another. One theory is that these people become beta-phenylethylamine "junkies," addicted to the changes in the body that take place when they fall in love.

Hysteroid dysphoria is the medical term doctors use to describe a type of depression that seems to fit the model of love addiction. In this syndrome, people (typically women) continually go through a cycle of falling in love, or seeking romantic attention, then becoming depressed when they break up or feel rejected. Many who suffer from this disorder eat chocolate when they feel depressed. This was an interesting observation for love addiction researchers. Chocolate naturally contains large amounts of beta-phenylethylamine. It would seem that these women are instinctively trying to replace the depleted supplies of the stimulant brain chemical. But there is some question about whether the PEA from chocolate actually reaches the brain in amounts large enough to help the mood or is instead simply digested and metabolized in the body.

Monoamine oxidase (MAO) is a type of brain enzyme that breaks down various neurotransmitters, including PEA, dopamine, and norepinephrine. Drugs called MAO inhibitors block the action of this enzyme and are used to treat depression. The drugs work by preventing the breakdown of the neurotransmitters, so that sufficient amounts of the euphoria chemicals remain in the brain. MAO inhibitors may be useful in treating love addiction as well.

Television

Ninety-eight percent of all American homes have television sets. Nearly half of these homes have two TV sets. Television has literally changed our society and the way we live. For parents, TV is a convenient babysitter. (The average child watches about twenty-four hours of television a week.) It's also an educator. Preschool children who watch education shows like *Sesame Street* often begin school with a better knowledge of numbers and of the alphabet.

Television is the number one form of relaxation for many people. After a hard day's work at school or at a job, all it takes is a flick of the switch, and you can sit back and be entertained.

But the "boob tube" has also been the object of controversy. Some feel that there is just too much violence on the TV screen. By the time a child is fifteen, he or she will have seen over 12,000 violent acts on TV. The violence we see on the screen desensitizes us to violence in the real world, and it becomes more accepted in our perception of the ways things are. TV has also been accused of sending mixed messages about sex.

Some people feel, however, that the messages on television aren't the only problem; television is a problem in and of itself. These people feel that television trains people not to think for themselves. There is no interaction with a TV set. When we read a book, we have to picture what the words are describing. Reading develops our imaginations and builds up skills in reasoning. When we watch something on television, though, there is nothing to interpret. The TV shows us everything in living color. TV watching has also been blamed for the short attention spans of many young people today. Commercials flash by in thirty seconds or less, and in fast-paced dramas the cuts from scene to scene hardly seem much longer; an entire lifetime may be lived in a thirty-minute episode. The habit of studying in front of the TV set further tends to fragment students' concentration.

Television also takes time away from interaction with family and friends. By the time the average teenager graduates from high school, he or she will have spent more time in front of the television set than in any other activity, except sleeping. Some fear that TV is contributing to a disintegration of the family and leading to an inability to interact with others.

Many people eagerly look forward to their favorite TV shows and plan their schedules around them. Watching television becomes a habit, a pattern that we look forward to—and for some people one that they can't do without. Some would say it becomes an addiction. In a 1977 book, *The Plug-In Drug,* Marie Winn tried to point out the similarities between television and mind-numbing drugs that cause users to become addicted. Her 1987 sequel, *Unplugging the Plug-In Drug,* urged parents and children to try to kick the habit for a month (or at least a week). November 1987 was declared "No-TV November" in an effort to spread this effort. Students of over 300 schools volunteered to give up watching television for a week in response to the campaign.

Research on the addictive effects of television has found that people who watch TV compulsively become anxious and depressed when they are alone with nothing to do, and they have a problem using free time productively. Others have found that, although there are many exceptions, television addicts generally do not do well in school.

Many kids who watch a lot of television (six or seven hours a day is a not uncommon total for some high school students) view their habit as something they should cut down on. They regard it as an addiction like cigarette smoking or drinking.

Heavy TV watchers are popularly described as "couch potatoes" because they typically lounge around on the couch eating snacks and watching TV. In January 1988 couch potatoes from around the country gathered together in Illinois, not to change their television habits but to celebrate their addiction, in the First Annual Couch Potato Convention.

The subject of television watching is one that is likely to be debated for a long time. Some see it as an important problem that affects us all. Others view it as a normal way of life. Watching occasional shows can be a healthy form of relaxation, but as in all addictions, when TV begins to rule your life and you can't enjoy other activities during your free time, you know you're watching too much.

Shopping

"Born to Shop", "Shop Till You Drop", and "When the going gets tough, the tough go shopping" are amusing and harmless bumper stickers. But shopping can sometimes be more than an amusing pastime or the purchasing of necessities. For some people, shopping is an escape, and it can become a strong compulsion with serious consequences. On the surface it might not appear to be as serious a problem as drug or alcohol dependency, but compulsive shopping can cause severe emotional and financial problems. If you don't have the bank account to go with your craving for new things, it's easy to get into financial trouble.

Two-thirds of those who seek help for compulsive shopping are women. Overspending is believed by psychologists to be a way of coping with underlying emotional problems. People overspend for a number of reasons. Most "shopaholics" are insecure and use shopping to feel better about themselves. Women shopaholics tend to buy clothes to make themselves feel more attractive. Men tend to go overboard picking up the tabs at meals and buying electronic gadgets. According to Janet Damon, author of the 1988 book *Shopaholics,* compulsive shoppers use shopping to boost their self-esteem by buying an image of power. Overspenders buy fancy things they can't afford to impress others. Thinking about things they are going to buy gives them something to look forward to. Others use shopping as a way of feeling confidence and control over their lives. Shopping provides a quick fix when a person is feeling anxious or depressed. Buying something new and different gives the shopping addict a temporary "high." However, this high soon wears off, the underlying anxiety or lack of self-esteem surfaces, and the shopaholic feels the burning desire to shop again.

Overspenders often don't really find pleasure in their compulsion. It is done to fulfill an emotional need or to relieve tension and stress. The compulsive shopper often feels guilty after going on a spending binge.

Shopping can be a healthy and good experience. It means we value ourselves enough to reward ourselves. But compulsive shoppers spend way beyond their means. Their need for new clothes or other tokens of reward comes before paying for necessities—car payments, the rent, even food. When they realize imminent financial disaster is likely, they still can't control the compulsion.

It is hard for shopaholics to resist temptation. Shopping gives people feelings of control and importance. Salespeople are attentive to their desires. TV commercial bombard them with pleas to spend, spend, spend! Even whole channels are devoted to at-home shopping. Catalogs filled with attractive consumer products fill their mailboxes, and consumers are encouraged to buy on credit—to buy things with money they don't have. Over 107 million Americans have credit cards, and it is not coincidence that more people are filing for personal bankruptcy now than ever before.

Credit cards are the biggest temptation for shopaholics. A credit card to a shopaholic is like a bottle of liquor to an alcoholic. It is not at all uncommon for a shopaholic to have several dozen credits cards and to actively use all of them. Most of the self-help groups that provide support for shopping addicts urge them to severely limit the use of "plastic money." Often shopaholics are advised to destroy their credit cards. Being unable to borrow for purchases is an effective way to limit spending.

An overspender should do more than resist compulsive shopping urges. It is important to discover the underlying emotional reasons for a shopping compulsion because if a shopaholic goes "cold turkey," unresolved emotional problems could vent themselves in other compulsions like overeating or drinking. Counseling and peer groups of recovering shopaholics can play a major role in fighting an addictive problem.

Treatment Options

Even these lesser-known addictions now have treatment possibilities. Both love and sex addiction, for example, were widely acknowledged by the mainstream by the 1970's. Robin Norwood's 1985 book *Women Who Love Too Much* gave rise to hundreds of self-help groups for women who become addicted to love. The groups form when ordinary people get together and follow Norwood's ten-step plan for recovery, which, like AA's twelve-step plan, begins with admitting the problem and encourages finding spirituality with a power higher than oneself.

In 1978 Sex Addicts Anonymous was founded in Minneapolis, Minnesota. Today that city has more than thirty groups to treat sex and love addiction, and similar AA-type groups are to be found all over the country. At one time, sex addiction was something that nice people didn't even talk about, much less admit to. Psychologist Patrick Carnes's 1983 book *Out of the Shadows: Understanding Sexual Addiction* helped to increase the public awareness of the problem.

Compulsive shoppers, too, are now offered options to overcome their addiction. Psychologists who specialize in compulsive behavior treat compulsive shoppers with therapy to help them build up self-esteem and discover the underlying conflicts and emotional problems responsible for the addiction. Once patients realize why they are acting the way they do, they can better control their compulsive urges.

Others find comfort in self-help groups such as Debtors Anonymous with 145 groups across the nation. Its goal is to help those who have gotten into debt because of overspending or credit-card abuse to get their lives and finances back in order.

The Consumer Credit Counseling Service is a nationwide nonprofit organization that helps people budget their money and pay off their debts, for a sliding-scale fee. Each year 200,000 people seek help from their 410 nonprofit counseling centers. Forty percent seek help in January and February, after the extravagant buying for Christmas.

Like most addictions, compulsive shopping may require a lifetime struggle for control. When the urge to shop arises, it is best to substitute other activities—preferably things that are pleasurable but do not cost money, such as taking a hot bath, a leisurely walk, or a drive (*not* to the nearest shopping mall). A good book or movie can also help the urge to pass.

Some other tips are recommended for helping to control a shopping habit that is getting out of control:

1. Tell someone you may have a problem with overspending. (Knowing someone else is aware of the problem can provide extra motivation for fighting temptation.)

2. Keep records of what you buy. It's easy to rationalize a purchase when you buy it, but harder to justify needless items when you have to write them down.

162

3. Wait before buying something you think you need. After leaving the store, you may realize you don't really need it after all.

4. Return merchandise you don't really need.

5. Make a list of what you need before you go to a store, and then stick to that list when you get there.

6. Set time limits on how long you may spend shopping.

7. Don't shop when you're tired and can't think rationally.

8. Join a self-help group and call a fellow member when you feel the urge to shop.

Further Reading

Exercise

Grant, Eleanor. "The Exercise Fix." *Psychology Today,* February, 1988, pp. 24–28.

Marbella, Jean. "Exercise Can Become an Unhealthy Obsession." *The Baltimore Sun Syndication,* September 3, 1988.

Melillo, Wendy. "Hormone levels linked to 'runner's high'." *The Washington Post Syndication,* May 31, 1988.

Love and Sex

Carpineto, Jane. *The Don Juan Dilemma: How Women Cope With Men Who Play The Field.* New York: Morrow, 1989.

Dougherty, Steve. "Addicted to Love." *People,* October 3, 1988, p. 125+.

Norwood, Robin. *Women Who Love Too Much.* New York: Pocket Books, 1985.

Trachtenberg, P. "The Man Who Couldn't Be Faithful." *Mademoiselle,* May, 1989, pp. 188–189+.

Television

Barlow, Geoffrey and Alison Hill, eds. *Video Violence and Children.* New York: St. Martin's Press, 1986.

Demers, David P. *Breaking Your Child's TV Addiction.* Minneapolis, Minn.: Marquette Books, 1989.

Winn, Marie. *Unplugging the Plug-In Drug.* New York: Penguin, 1987.

Shopping

Damon, Janet E. *Shopaholics: Serious Help for Addicted Spenders.* Los Angeles: Price, Stern, Sloan Inc., 1988.

Reilly, Jean. "Seduced by the Power of Plastic." *People,* March 14, 1988, p. 115+.

Silver, Marc. "Curing Kids Who Want It All." *U.S. News & World Report,* March 20, 1989, pp. 83–85.

Helpful Organizations

Emotions Anonymous
P.O. Box 4245
Saint Paul, MN 55104
(612) 647-9712

Golden Valley Health Center
(800) 321-2273

National Association on Sex Addiction Problems
(800) 622-9494

Sex Addicts Anonymous
Twin Cities S.A. A.
P.O. Box 3038
Minneapolis, MN 55403

Sexaholics Anonymous
General Services Office
Box 300
Simi Valley, CA 93062

Sex and Love Addicts Anonymous
P.O. Box 88
New Town Branch
Boston, MA 02258

Spender Menders
P.O. Box 15000-156
San Francisco, CA 94115

EPILOGUE

Addiction and the Family

Alcoholism has been called the "family disease" because when a person has a drinking problem, it is likely to affect not only himself or herself but family members as well. As many as twenty million children in America live with a parent who drinks too much, and seven million children under the age of eighteen live with an alcoholic parent. Alcohol abuse is the largest single cause of family problems and is responsible for up to half of all family violence. A 1987 Gallup poll found that one family in four experienced a problem with alcohol abuse.

It can be very hard to live with an alcoholic—or, for that matter, with any addict. Life is confusing and unpredictable, for the addict cannot be depended on to react rationally. His or her reactions will be colored by the particular mix of chemicals in the blood and brain. Children may be praised or criticized for the same action at different times; they never know what to expect, and they grow up with a distorted view of the world.

Family members feel a complex mixture of emotions toward the addict. Children may live in fear of sudden, unprovoked beatings, yet may come to believe that the abuse was somehow their own fault. Anger at the parent's unfair actions may blend with feelings of guilt, and then the anger may be repressed. The family members of an addict may try to deny that a serious problem exists and typically hide the "family secret," pretending to outsiders that everything is normal. When the addiction is to an illegal drug, the child will feel the additional stress of divided loyalties as the needs of the family conflict with what is learned in school. Is it "moral" for a child to report a drug-abusing parent to the police? Some government officials have suggested that it is, and yet the result may be the jailing of the parent and total disruption of the family.

Codependents

Husbands, wives, and children, as well as others who live with or love an addict, may be forced into the role of desperately holding things together in spite of the addict's irresponsibility. They may attempt to control or manipulate the addict's behavior—generally, in vain. Their own frustration and repressed anger grow, and their own lives become disrupted by the addiction, even though they themselves are not addicts. Addiction specialists speak of such family members as *codependents* and are gradually recognizing that they may be as much in need of help as the addict.

Codependents may confront the addict, ignore the problem, or try to cover it up so that outsiders will not find out about it. They may argue and plead with the addict, who usually reacts by denying that a problem even exists.

Experts feel that the best approach for the family is to let the addict cope with the results of his or her own indulgence; only by actually feeling the pain of "hitting bottom" will the addict realize he or she needs help. Trying to control the addict by scolding, threatening, nagging, pleading, or making him or her feel guilty usually doesn't work. Neither does trying to cover up and protect the addict by taking care of his or her responsibilities. Protective behaviors like these are called *enabling behaviors* because they provide the addict with an excuse to continue the addictive actions. Calling in "sick" for an alcoholic who is nursing a hangover, lending a drug addict money that will be used to buy the next fix, or paying the debts of a compulsive gambler merely shield him or her from the damaging effects of the addiction. This kind of "help" just delays the time when the addict will recognize the need for real help. It's that much easier to keep drinking, gambling, or using drugs because the addict expects to be protected and looked after. Nagging or trying to control the addict just supplies another excuse. (" Of course I drink! You'd drink, too, if you had to live with all that nagging.")

Eventually the codependents begin to realize that their own lives must come first. Only the addict can take the steps to bring the addiction under control; nothing that family members can do or say will force the addict to do so until he or she is ready to acknowledge the problem.

The Family's Role in Rehabilitation

Alcoholism and other addictions cannot be cured, but they can be controlled. But an addict may make many false starts and suffer many relapses in the struggle to conquer the addiction. Some think that when they stop briefly, they've proven they can stop when they want to, so they really don't have a problem. But their lives remain a mess, and the rest of the family suffers too.

It is important for the entire family to be involved in a recovering addict's rehabilitation, regardless of what kind of treatment plan is chosen. Studies of teenage addicts, for example, have found that kids whose parents get involved in the rehabilitation are ten times more likely to be rehabilitated. Other studies indicate that without family encouragement the rehabilitation rate drops to 2 to 3 percent success!

When the addict returns home from treatment, it is important that the family does not fall back into the same patterns. It may be necessary for the family to get help in resolving their feelings of anger or hurt.

It will be difficult enough for the recovering addict, who will be under constant pressure to stay straight. He or she may also feel like an outcast, for it will be necessary to give up old friends and an old environment that could trigger a return to drug use. The resulting feelings of dejection and loneliness can make going back to drugs more appealing. While the rehabilitated addict develops new interests and works out new ways of dealing with problems without the crutch of drugs, having family members to turn to for sympathy and advice can be an enormous help.

Needs of the Codependents

Even if the addict won't go for help, family members can be helped to lead better lives. Al-Anon is a support group for families of alcoholics to help them cope with the problems of living with an alcoholic. Alateen is a support group specifically for young people with an alcoholic parent or friend. There are similar support groups for families of other types of addicts, such as Gam-Anon for codependents of compulsive gamblers. In the past, social workers and counselors were concerned only with curing the addict, and the family was not really considered. Today the idea of codependency is stressed in alcohol and other addiction programs because addiction affects the entire family.

Children who grow up in an addict's household may have special problems when they become adults. Adult children of alcoholics (now referred to as ACOA's by health professionals) still carry much of the hurt and other destructive emotions they felt as children, and they may still be using some of the warped coping mechanisms they had learned in order to survive in their chaotic families. Many of them are unable to express emotions normally or to trust others enough to form loving relationships. Some compensate for the lack of appreciation they experienced as children by becoming overachievers or caregivers, roles they maintain at a cost of great internal stress. Many ACOA's form relationships with addicts, unconsciously recreating the painful yet familiar conditions of their childhood. A distressing 60 percent of ACOA's become alcoholics themselves! There are now a number of special treatment groups for ACOA's, to help them come to grips with the feelings they have kept bottled up, which still affect their lives.

Further Reading

Beattie, Melody. *Codependent No More.* New York: Harper & Row, 1987.

McConnell, Patty. *A Workbook for Healing: Adult Children of Alcoholics.* San Francisco: Harper & Row, 1986.

Sexias, Judith and Geraldine Youcha. *Children of Alcoholism: A Survivor's Manual.* New York: Crown, 1985.

Shapiro, Joseph P. "How To Beat Drugs." *U.S. News & World Report,* September 11, 1989, pp. 69–81.

Helpful Organizations

Adult Children of Alcoholics
Torrence, CA
(213) 534-1815

Al-Anon Family Group
115 E 23 St
New York, NY 10010
(800) 344-2666

Co-Dependents Anonymous
Phoenix, AZ
(602) 944-0141

Hale House Center
68 Edgecomb Ave
New York, NY 10030
(212) 690-5623

Treatment of Addictions

Researchers hope that some day our growing knowledge of the brain and its biochemistry will yield true cures for addiction—ways of rebuilding defective nerve structures and counteracting the chemical reactions that lead to cravings for drugs. That day is still far off. There are no cures for addiction yet, but we do have a number of ways to treat various addictions and bring them under control. The victory over addiction is not won in a single glorious battle; it is a long, drawn-out war that must be fought and refought for the rest of the addict's life.

The first step toward bringing addiction under control must be taken by the addict—deciding that he or she *wants* to be treated and is willing to take an active part in the struggle. For a long time, people who worked with alcoholics and other addicts believed that for a real commitment to be made, the addict must first "hit bottom"—be faced with the worst of human misery. Usually hitting bottom meant becoming a homeless "street person," who had lost connections with friends and loved ones and lived only for the next fix, which might be obtained by begging, stealing, or prostitution.

What a waste of human lives! The addict loses family and friends and perhaps a promising career and, in the process, may do terrible harm to others. An Amtrak train collided with three Conrail engines near Baltimore in 1987, killing fifteen people and injuring 175; blood tests afterward revealed that the Conrail engineer and brakeman had both been taking drugs.

Doctors have one of the highest rates of alcoholism and drug abuse of any occupational group. That distressing statistic is understandable in view of the terrible stress under which doctors live and work, continually making life-and-death decisions; it is all too easy for them to slip a few pills or a vial of liquid out of a hospital dispensary or write a prescription for a controlled substance. The problem of impaired doctors is a tragic one for the individual addicts; but what about their patients? How many have died or suffered needlessly because a doctor's judgment was dulled or reactions slowed by the action of addictive drugs?

Instead of waiting for an addict to "hit bottom" by himself or herself, concerned family or friends may be able to save time—and reduce the damage—through a technique called *intervention*. Family members and friends rehearse beforehand how they are going to present the situation and then confront the addict. Each person tells the addict how drug use has affected their relationship. They affirm that they care, and they urge the user to get help.

Intervention helps to overwhelm the drug user. It makes him or her realize that the problem is not a secret and that people care. Seeking help from a treatment program is a big decision, and the shock of the confrontation and the feeling of support from people important in the addict's life can be a big help.

Treatment Approaches

The first step in a treatment program is often *detoxification*—getting the drugs out of the person's body and coping with any withdrawal symptoms that may occur. Some programs use various medications to ease the transition; a high intake of candy and other carbohydrate sources may also help to soothe the protesting brain cells. But some programs require the addict to quit "cold turkey"—complete withdrawal of all drugs. The theory is that the suffering during withdrawal will provide an unforgettable lesson and help to strengthen the addict against resuming drug use.

Some treatment programs provide a substitute drug that will help the addict to stay off the "drug of choice"—the methadone maintenance programs for heroin addicts, for example. Others stress complete *abstinence,* refraining from taking any addictive drugs at all. (It is all too easy for a recovering addict to slip into an addiction to a different substance when the drug of choice is forbidden. That was why, for example, Mets pitcher Dwight Gooden was required by his rehabilitation program for cocaine abuse to abstain from all illegal drugs and alcoholic beverages as well. An innocent couple of beers with the guys could be the ticket back to addiction.)

Many treatment programs focus on various types of *behavior modification,* training the addict to unlearn old habits of abuse and learn new, healthier ways of living. The *aversion* approach links the addictive behavior with some very unpleasant experiences. For example, an alcoholic may be given an electric shock when he or she takes a drink, or may take a drug that induces vomiting if it is combined with alcohol intake. Hypnosis is another technique sometimes employed to provide the addict with extra motivation to abstain.

Whatever approach is used, it is generally combined with some form of psychological counseling to uncover the problems that prompted the use of drugs and to teach the addict more effective ways of coping with life. One-on-one individual therapy or group therapy may be used. Many addiction specialists feel that a group of addicts, sharing their experiences and struggles, can provide important mutual support. This is the basis of many programs such as Alcoholics Anonymous that can help sustain the addict in efforts to lead a drug-free life.

It won't be easy to stay drug free after completing the treatment. The U.S. Office of Technology Assessment says that two out of three who enter treatment for drug or alcohol rehabilitation will recover. Other estimates are much lower—some suggest that only 20 to 50 percent remain drug free.

One of the problems with treatment programs is that people differ in the way they respond to various programs, and it is impossible to know beforehand which type will work for a particular individual. It is not uncommon for an addict to try out several different programs before finding one that works best for him or her.

Drug treatment programs can also be expensive. Some health insurance policies cover some of the cost, which may help to guide a decision.

One reason that addicts often go back to drug use is that addiction is not simply a matter of the effects of the drug on the brain and body. There is a whole complicated interaction of habits and associations. Leaving the unprotected atmosphere of the treatment program, the addict is typically plunged back into the old environment where the dependence started. The problems that the addict had been trying to escape may still exist and be even more difficult to face when the crutch of the addiction is removed. An alcoholic may have few friends other than "drinking buddies", and they may urge, "Aw, just one drink won't hurt." Particular activities may have been linked with the addiction: A smoker, for example, may have been in the habit of having a cigarette immediately after awakening, another after breakfast; talking on the telephone, reading the paper, and other daily activities may have been part of the smoking pattern. After quitting, the former smoker may feel the craving all over again each time one of these familiar activities occurs.

Some of the most effective treatment programs focus on overcoming relapses. The traditional view was that once an addict slips, he or she is doomed to fall back into the old addictive pattern. A recovering alcoholic who is persuaded to take "just one drink," for example, may think, "What the heck, I'm off the wagon anyway; I might as well have a few more." The new view regards slips as emergencies that are potentially dangerous but can also become valuable learning experiences. A slip is an error in learning, not a failure in willpower, says University of Washington psychologist Alan

Marlatt, who notes that about 20 percent of the people can kick a habit on the first try but most need several attempts. He provides his patients with a card to carry, listing tactics for coping with slips that include:

1. Treat each slip as an emergency requiring immediate action.
2. Remember that a slip is not a relapse.
3. Renew your commitment.
4. Review the actions that led to the lapse so you won't repeat them.
5. Make an immediate plan for recovery.
6. Ask someone for help.

Having a friend (or a psychologist) one can call in an emergency for advice, encouragement, and sympathy can also be a great help. Many of the successful programs such as Alcoholics Anonymous provide for such a buddy system to aid the recovering addict.

The Future of Addiction Treatment

We are not doing very well in the drug war so far, and the current treatment approaches are not effective even for all of the addicts who are motivated enough to try them. The prospect of a lifetime struggle against one's own urges and inner cravings may seem dismal.

We are making progress, though. The experience built up through treatment and mutual support programs is slowly pointing out the techniques that work best. Meanwhile, researchers are gradually discovering how the brain works, down to the level of its biochemical reactions. UCLA medical professor and associate dean Stanley G. Korenman has predicted that a well-funded research program could reveal the biochemical details of all the major addictions within ten to fifteen years. With that knowledge, he says, we could design treatments to reverse the harmful effects of the drugs and also the addictive cravings.

Our progress on the biochemical front is opening up another possibility as well. We might be able to win people away from illegal, harmful, addictive drugs by devising better drugs that produce pleasurable effects without damaging the brain and body. How much of a market would there be for dangerous and expensive illegal drugs if safe, nonaddictive drugs were readily available?

If scientists do devise such drugs, would it be ethical to produce and distribute them? Should we encourage a society in which people pop pills to stay happy. Many people would say no. And yet, many of those same people drink coffee, tea, or cola beverages; many of them smoke or indulge in occasional "social drinking"; many of them buy lottery tickets or take part in bingo games.

New Jersey chemist Frederic H. Megson makes an interesting case for the alternative:

> "One football player related that a shot of cocaine gave him the same feeling as a 70-yard touchdown run. I would like to have that thrill, but at my age I can never hope to enjoy it on the field. I shall not attempt to achieve it via the present drugs because, aside from their being illegal, their side effects are so very harmful to the body. The thrill itself is no more harmful than the much milder 'high' one enjoys in finding an unusually beautiful shell at the beach . . . . It is my hope that through research by pharmaceutical chemists, with government encouragement, the cocaine molecule (or a related one) can be modified to remove the harmful side effects, as has been done with numerous medicines. An alternative is to create new compounds with similar desirable effects, but which are much less harmful and much less addictive."

Ronald K. Siegel, a drug researcher at the UCLA School of Medicine, contends that humans (and animals, as well) have an inherent need to seek mood-altering chemicals from time to time. "We need intoxicants", he says, "—not in the sense that an addict needs a fix, but because the need is as much a part of the human condition as sex, hunger, and thirst." He proposes an

178

all-out effort to win the drug war by designing ideal drugs that would combine positive effects such as stimulation or pleasure with virtually no toxic effects or unwanted side effects. They would have built-in controls to limit the time of their action and prevent excessive use or overdoses—that is, they would not be addictive.

Molecular chemists are not yet able to fine tune drug effects to that degree, but they are rapidly gaining the skills that may one day make it possible to design such ideal drugs. Some drug specialists agree that such a goal would be desirable, but many others are more dubious. Andrew Weil, of the University of Arizona College of Medicine, for example, warns that we may never be able to design a perfect drug that would not interfere with psychological and spiritual growth and would not have the potential for dependence. Herbert Kleber, deputy director of the Office of National Drug Control Policy, commented, "I can only note that all previous attempts along this line have ended in disaster."

Whether we wish only to cure addiction or attempt to develop a harmless, "perfect drug," Stanley Korenman's call for a massive program of basic research into addiction seems the most promising approach. In his words: "The laboratory must be a principal battleground for a successful war on drugs."

Further Reading

Beaty, Jonathan. "Do Humans Need to Get High." *Time,* August 21, 1989, p. 58.

Chiauzzi, Emil, Ph.D. "Breaking the Patterns that Lead to Relapse." *Psychology Today,* December 1989, pp. 18–19.

Goleman, Daniel. "Breaking Bad Habits: New Therapy Focuses on the Relapse." *New York Times,* December 27, 1988.

Lasater, Lane. *Recovery from Compulsive Behavior.* Deerfield Beach, Fla.: Health Communications, Inc., 1988.

Leerhsen, Charles. "Unite and Conquer." *Newsweek*, February 5, 1990, pp. 50–55.

Johnson, Vernon. *Intervention: How to Help Someone Who Doesn't Want Help.* Minneapolis: Johnson Institute, 1986.

Siegel, Ronald K., PhD. *Intoxication: Life in Pursuit of Artificial Paradise.* New York: Crown, 1988.

Timmons, Tim and Steve Arterburn. *Hooked on Life: How to Totally Recover from Addictions & Dependency.* Nashville, Tenn.: Oliver-Nelson, 1989.

Helpful Organizations

The following agencies will provide free information on addresses and telephone numbers of support groups for help with specific problems:

California Self-Help Center
405 Hilgard Avenue
Los Angeles, CA 90024
(213) 825-1799

Illinois Self-Help Center
1600 Dodge Avenue
Suite S-122
Evanston, IL 60201
(312) 328-0470

**Massachusetts Clearinghouse
of Mutual Help Groups**
113 Skinner Hall, U. of Mass.
Amherst, MA 01003
(413) 545-2313

**Minnesota Mutual Help
Resource Center**
919 Lafond Avenue
St. Paul, MN 55104
(612) 642-4060

National Self-Help Clearinghouse
33 West 42nd Street
New York, NY 10036
(212) 642-2944

**Self-Help Clearinghouse
of Greater Washington**
100 N. Washington Street
Falls Church, VA 22046
(703) 536-4100

Type of Drug	Examples	Street Names	Comes From	Legal Status	Medical Uses	How Taken
Depressants:						
Alcohol	Beer Liquor Wine		grain grain fruit	not controlled, must be 21 in most states.	none	swallowed
Barbituates	Nembutal Phenobarbital Seconal Amytal	downers	synthetic	controlled	insomnia, tension, epileptic seizures	swallowed
Other Depressants	Methaqua-lone Chloral Hydrate	quaalude, ludes	synthetic	illegal controlled	none insomnia	swallowed
Inhalants	Aerosols Airplane glue Amyl nitrate Butyl nitrate Nitrous oxide	freon poppers, snappers locker room	synthetic	not controlled	none none dilate blood vessels anesthetic	sniffed
Narcotics	Codeine Demerol Heroin Methadone Morphine Opium Percodan	dope, horse, junk, smack	Opium poppy synthetic Opium poppy synthetic Opium poppy Opium poppy synthetic	controlled controlled illegal controlled controlled controlled	cough pain none w/d from heroin pain pain, diarrhea pain	inj., swa. inj., swa. inj., smo., sni. inj., swa. inj., smo., swa. smo., swa.

Psych.Dep.	Phys.Dep	Tolerance	How It Feels	How It Works	Harmful Effects	Withdrawal
Yes	Yes	Yes	relaxation, breakdown of inhibitions, impairs coordination, euphoria, decreased alertness	depresses central nervous system (CNS) through GABA	Overdose: nausea, unconsciousness, hangover, death Long Term Abuse: malnutrition, psychosis, liver and brain damage, death	headache, cramps, nausea, jumpiness, tremors, shakes, hallucinations, convulsions, delerium tremors, death possible
Yes	Yes	Yes	relaxation, euphoria, decreased alertness, impaired coordination, drowsiness	depresses CNS through neurotransmitter GABA	disturbed sleep Overdose: slurred speech, stupor, hangover, death Long Term Abuse: sleepiness, confusion, irritability	sweating, cramps, nausea, seizures, convulsions, hallucinations
Yes	Yes	Yes	relaxation, euphoria, decreased alertness	depresses CNS		
Yes	Maybe	Yes	relaxation, euphoria, impaired coordination	depresses CNS	nosebleed, hallucinations, confusion Overdose: stupor, death Long Term Abuse: damage to: liver, kidney, bone marrow, brain, death	nausea, depression, insomnia
Yes	Yes	Yes	relaxation, relief of pain and anxiety, euphoria, drowsiness, decreased alertness, hallucinations	binds to brain endorphin centers	Overdose: stupor, death Long Term Abuse: lethargy, weight loss, temporary impotence, withdrawal sickness	watery eyes, runny nose, loss of appetite, irritability, tremors, panic, chills, sweating, cramps, nausea

183

Type of Drug	Examples	Street Names	Comes From	Legal Status	Medical Uses	How Taken
Tranquilizers	Benzo-diazepines	Librium Valium Xanax	synthetic	controlled	alcohol detox, alcoholism, anxiety, psychosis	swallowed
	Meprobamate	Miltown				swallowed
	Thorazine					swallowed
Stimulants						
Amphetamines		uppers, pep pills	synthetic	controlled	depression, hyperactivity, narcolepsy, weight control	injected, swallowed
	Benzedrine	bennies				
	Dexedrine					
	Methedrine	speed, ice				
	Preludin					
Antidepress-ants	Tricyclics	Elavil, Tofranil	synthetic	controlled	anxiety, depression	injected, swallowed
Caffeine	Coffee		coffee bean	not controlled	fatigue, headache	swallowed
	Cola		kola nut			
	No-Doz		synthetic			
	Tea		tea leaves			

184

Psych. Dep.	Phys. Dep.	Tolerance	How It Feels	How It Works	Harmful Effects	Withdrawal
Yes	Yes	Yes	relief of anxiety and tension, sleep	binds to brain benzodiazepine receptors; interaction with GABA	Overdose: drowsiness, blurred vision, dizziness, stupor Long Term Abuse: destroys blood cells, jaundice, coma, death	dysphoria, insomnia, cramps, vomiting, sweating, tremors, convulsions
Maybe	Yes	Yes	increased alertness, excitment, euphoria, decreased appetite	through dopamine	Overdose: restlessness, rapid speech, irritability, insomnia, convulsions, possilble death Long Term Abuse: insomnia, delusion, hallucinations, psychosis	apathy, long periods of sleep, irritabilty, depression, disorientation
Maybe	Yes	Yes	relief of anxiety and depression	blocks reuptake of serotonin & norepinephrine	Overdose: nausea, hypertension, weight loss, insomnia Long Term Abuse: stupor, coma, convulsions, heart failure, death	nausea, headache, malaise after abrupt stopping
Yes	Maybe	Yes	increased alertness	stimulates CNS	Overdose: restlessness, insomnia, upset stomach Long Term Abuse: may contribute to heart disease and cancer	headache, irritability, sleepiness, sluggishness, nausea

Type of Drug	Examples	Street Names	Comes From	Legal Status	Medical Uses	How Taken
Cocaine	Cocaine	coke, snow, flack, Big C	coca leaves	controlled	local anesthetic	injected, smoked, sniffed
	Crack	base, rock	coca leaves (freebase mixed with baking soda)		none	
	Basuco	bazooka, diesel	coca leaves (crude base)			
Methylphen-idate	Ritalin		synthetic	controlled	hyperactivity, narcolepsy	injected, swallowed
Nicotine	Cigarettes Cigars Pipes Snuff Chewing tobacco		tobacco leaves	not controlled, must be 18 in most states	none (insecticide)	smoked smoked smoked sniffed chewed

Psych. Dep.	Phys. Dep.	Tolerance	How It Feels	How It Works	Harmful Effects	Withdawal
Yes	Yes	Yes	exhiliration, excitation, tremors	stimulates CNS through dopamine & norepinephrine	Overdose: irritability, depression, psychosis, death (stroke/heart attack) Long Term Abuse: nosebleeds, headache, twiches, convulsions, psychosis, death; Basuco: lead poising	"crash": apathy, long periods of sleep, irritablity, depression, disorientation
Yes	Yes	Yes	increased alertness, euphoria	CNS stimulant	nervousness, insomnia Overdose: vomiting, agitaton, convulsions, hallucination Long Term Abuse: psychosis	severe depression
Yes	Maybe	Yes	relaxation, constriction of blood vessels	stimulates CNS by mimicking adrenaline & acetylcholine, stimulates endorphins	Overdose: headache, loss of appetite, nausea Long Term Abuse: breathing impairment, heart and lung disease, cancer, death	insomnia, hyperactivity, decreased appetite

Type of Drug	Examples	Street Names	Comes From	Legal Status	Medical Uses	How Taken
Psychedelics:						
Cannabis	Hashish	hash	Cannabis plant	illegal	none	smoked, swallowed
	Marijuana	pot, grass, weed, reefer, herb,smoke, MaryJane, Acapulco gold	Cannabis plant		under investigation for headache, tension, poor appetite, glaucoma; suppresses vomiting in cancer chemotherapy	smoked, swallowed
	THC (tetrahydro-cannabinol)		synthetic			injected, swallowed
Hallucinogens	DMT		synthetic	illegal	none	smoked
	LSD	acid	synthetic	illegal	none	inj., swa.
	Mescaline	mesc	cactus, peyote	illegal	none	swallowed
	Nutmeg		nutmeg tree	not controlled		sni., swa.
	PCP (phen-cyclidine)	angel dust	synthetic	illegal	veterinary anesthetic	inj., smo., swa.
	Psilocybin		Psilocybe mushroom	illegal	none	swallowed
	Scopolamine		Henbane plant or synthetic	controlled	cough, intestinal spasms	swallowed
	STP		synthetic	illegal	none	swallowed
Designer Drugs	MDMA	ecstasy	synthetic ampheta-mines	controlled	psychiatric therapy (promotes empathy)	swallowed
	MDEA	eve				

Psych. Dep.	Phys. Dep.	Tolerance	How It Feels	How It Works	Harmful Effects	Withdawal
Yes		Yes	relaxation, breakdown of inhibitions, euphoria, altered perception and judgement	depresses CNS (THC remains in brain for a week or more)	reddening of eyes, increased heartbeat Overdose: panic,stupor Long Term Abuse: fatigue, psychosis, memory problems, reduced sexual potency, lung cancer	insomnia, hyperactivity, decreased appetite, flulike symptoms
No No No		Maybe Yes Yes	perceptual changes, excitation, hallucinations, exhilarations	acts on locus coeruleus in brain, and on serotonin receptors	Overdose: anxiety, exhaustion, vomiting, psychosis, death Long Term Abuse: delusions, panic, psychosis, possible flashbacks	
	Yes	Yes				PCP: depression, suicidal feelings, paranoia, violence
No		Maybe	panic	anticholinergic		
			euphoria	stimulates serotonin release	increased heart-rate & blood pressure, sweating, chills, confusion, anxiety, nausea, depression, brain damage Overdose: death	

189

Index